EL PISTOLERO
LUIS
SUAREZ

Also by Tom and Matt Oldfield:

Alexis Sánchez: The Wonder Boy

Eden Hazard: The Boy in Blue

Gareth Bale: The Boy Who Became a Galáctico

Wayne Rooney: Captain of England

Raheem Sterling: Young Lion

EL PISTOLERO
LUIS
SUAREZ

TOM AND MATT OLDFIELD

DINO

Published by Dino Books,
an imprint of John Blake Publishing Ltd,
3 Bramber Court, 2 Bramber Road,
London W14 9PB, England

www.johnblakebooks.com

www.facebook.com/johnblakebooks ▌f▐
twitter.com/jblakebooks ▌t▐

This edition published in 2016

ISBN: 978 1 78 606 012 9

British Library Cataloguing-in-Publication Data:

A catalogue record for this book is available from the British Library.

Design by www.envydesign.co.uk
Cover illustration by Dan Leydon
Background image: Shutterstock

Printed in Great Britain by CPI Group (UK) Ltd

3 5 7 9 10 8 6 4

Papers used by John Blake Publishing are natural, recyclable products made from
wood grown in sustainable forests. The manufacturing processes conform to the
environmental regulations of the country of origin.

Every attempt has been made to contact the relevant copyright-holders, but some
were unobtainable. We would be grateful if the appropriate people could contact us.

For Noah and the future Oldfields to come
Looking forward to reading this book together

TABLE OF CONTENTS

ACKNOWLEDGEMENTS

This was a very special opportunity for us, as brothers, to work together on something we are both so passionate about. Football has always been a big part of our lives. We hope this book will inspire others to start – or continue – playing football and chasing their dreams.

Writing a book like this was one of our dreams, and we are extremely thankful to John Blake Publishing and James Hodgkinson and Chris Mitchell, in particular, for making this project possible. It was great to have your guidance and support throughout our writing process.

We are also grateful to all the friends and family that encouraged us along the way. Your interest and sense of humour helped to keep us on track. Will, Doug, Mills, John, James Pang-Oldfield and the rest of our King Edward VI friends, our aunts, uncles, cousins, the Nottingham and Montreal families and so many others – thank you all.

Melissa, we could not have done this without your understanding and support. Thank you for being as excited about this collaboration as we were. Iona, thank you for your kindness and encouragement during long, work-filled weekends.

Noah, we're doing our best to make football your favourite sport! We look forward to reading this book with you in the years ahead.

Mum and Dad, the biggest 'thank you' is reserved for you. You introduced us to football and then devoted hours and hours to taking us to games. You bought the tickets, the kits, the boots. We love football because you encouraged us to. Thank you for all the love, all the laughs and for always believing in us. This book is for you.

CHAPTER 1

CHAMPION OF EUROPE

6 June 2015. As Luis took a quick glance around the stadium, all he saw were the colours of Barcelona. It was still thirty minutes before kick-off but they were cheering as if the warm-up was the real thing. He stretched out his right leg, loosening the muscles and preparing his body for the biggest game of his life.

Xavi fired the ball towards him, catching him by surprise, and Luis turned to chase it as it rolled off the pitch. As he crossed the touchline, almost within touching distance of the Barcelona fans in the front row, all he heard was 'Suárez! Suárez!' He grinned and gave the fans a quick wave. They were ready for this Champions League Final – and so was he.

Hard times make you appreciate the good times – that had been Luis's motto over the past year. After all the anger, the tears, the headlines and the four-month suspension, he had bounced back better than ever. There was nothing he could do about his mistakes in the past, except try to learn from them. He had shut out all the distractions and focused on only two things: football and family. Now, having already won the Spanish league title and the Spanish Cup, he was ninety minutes away from completing an amazing Treble.

Back in the dressing room, Dani Alves turned the music up loud and the players tried their best to relax. Luis walked over to the far side, where the 'Suárez 9' shirt was hanging. He had worn that name and number plenty of times but it had never looked better than it did now. He looked up at the countdown timer high on the wall – less than fifteen minutes to go. He put on the shirt, pulled up his socks and slotted in a tiny pair of shin pads. Their opponents, Juventus, would play a physical style, but Luis had never liked big, bulky shin pads. He could handle the kicks.

'Dani, throw me the tape,' he called.

'Do I work for you now?' Dani replied, laughing. 'Just because you score the goals, you think you run the place?'

Luis had quickly built good friendships within the Barcelona squad. For the first time since leaving Uruguay, he was surrounded by teammates who spoke Spanish, and that had certainly helped him to settle in quickly. He still had to pinch himself to believe that he was scoring goals alongside a magician like Lionel Messi.

The referee knocked on the dressing-room door. It was time. Luis finished putting the tape round his wrist, jumped to his feet and joined in the quick high fives. As they headed for the tunnel, he felt a hand on his shoulder and turned to see Xavi waiting with some final words of advice. 'Stay calm out there. They know all about your temper and they'll be trying to wind you up. Play your game and ignore them. We need you.'

Luis nodded. Many of the things he regretted most in his football career were related to reckless moments on the pitch. He just needed to win every game, and sometimes he went too far. 'Don't worry. I won't let you guys down,' he added with a serious face. Then a grin broke out. 'After the game, it'll just be my goals that people are talking about.'

For most of his teammates, this was yet another Champions League Final. But it was Luis's first and he was shaking with a combination of nerves and excitement. The atmosphere was incredible – the anthem, the fans, the perfect pitch. It was like no other game he had ever played.

As he passed the ball around in a little triangle with Messi and Neymar, he had no doubts about the result of the game. With all their star players, how could they not score three or four goals? He placed the ball in the centre circle. He would be getting the first touch of the final! When the whistle blew for kick-off, Luis felt like he could run all day.

Barcelona took an early lead and Juventus equalised in the second half, but Luis struggled to find his best form. Was it just the big occasion that was getting to him? He worked hard but nothing was falling for him. With twenty-five minutes to go, he even feared that he might be substituted. Clapping his hands, he urged his teammates to do more, saying, 'Leo, let's go. Let's make something happen.'

One of Luis's biggest strengths was that he never gave up and always believed that a chance would come his way. From his earliest years, he just knew where to be at the right moment to score goals. There's still time, he told himself. Things can change in a second.

Then it happened. Messi dribbled past three Juventus defenders, and Luis saw his teammate preparing to take a shot. His instincts took over. He wasn't going to watch the shot. As soon as Messi pulled his leg back to shoot, Luis was racing towards the goal, looking for a rebound. Juventus goalkeeper Gianluigi Buffon made the save but the ball bounced loose. None of the defenders had a chance. Luis was too quick. Before they could move, he had pounced on the ball and fired a shot into the top corner.

Suddenly, as the emotions took over, everything was a blur. He jumped over the advertising boards onto the athletics track that surrounded the pitch. Lionel, Neymar, Dani and the rest of his teammates joined him, climbing on his back and burying him in hugs. He had saved the day. 'That was such a classic Suárez goal,' Dani yelled. 'You shoot, you score – that's why you're El Pistolero!'

As he jogged back to the halfway line, Luis couldn't stop smiling. He loved scoring in big finals. From the first time he kicked a ball, he had always wanted to be the goalscorer and the hero. While the game was stopped for a substitution, he allowed his mind to wander, just for a minute, back to his beloved Uruguay, where it all began.

CHAPTER 2

LEARNING THE BASE-ICS

'I'll be back for dinner,' Paolo called to his parents as he opened the door. 'I've got to go. My friends are waiting.'

Hearing his brother's voice, Luis leapt off his bed and raced into the hallway. 'Wait! Are you going to the football pitches? Can I come with you?'

Paolo turned and looked at his little brother. He had excitement all over his face. Luis always wanted to play football with the older boys but every time he was told he was too young. Today, Paolo was feeling generous.

'Okay, but don't say anything silly in front of my friends. And you'll have to be careful. The other boys are all ten or eleven. Don't get hurt.'

'Don't worry,' Luis replied, with a toothy grin. 'I can look after myself.'

Paolo couldn't help but laugh. His little brother couldn't even tie his own shoelaces but he was fearless.

The Suárez family lived just outside the army base, where Luis's father, Rodolfo, was a soldier. Ever since they had moved in, Luis had heard the stories about the pitches on the base and the endless football matches after school each day. Finally, he would get to see it for himself. He ran to the door before Paolo could change his mind.

The base was even bigger and better than he had pictured. As they turned a corner, past a large 'Military zone, No entry' sign, four football pitches magically appeared. Boys and girls were running around on all of them. Like Luis, most of them were barefoot, chasing balls that looked like they were one bad bounce away from being useless.

Paolo found his friends and, with a little embarrassment, explained that little Luis was here to play as well.

'He's three years old,' one of the boys sneered.
'Can he even run?'

'I'm four,' Luis fired back. 'And I'm fast.' That
made the whole group laugh.

They picked teams. Luis was just told to join
Paolo's team. 'Stay out of trouble,' Paolo warned,
pointing for Luis to stay out on the far side of the
pitch, away from the action.

'No chance,' Luis mumbled to himself. He had
waited long enough for this moment. He wanted an
up-close view.

At first, he was too busy watching everything –
how fast the older boys could run, how hard they
kicked the ball, how small he felt on such a big pitch.

Suddenly, the ball was coming towards him,
with three boys sprinting after it. For a second, Luis
wanted to run away. But he didn't. He stuck out
his foot to stop the ball and then, without looking,
kicked it as hard as he could. Luckily, it went straight
to Paolo. 'Nice one,' shouted Pedro, one of the best
players in the group. Luis felt ten feet tall.

For what felt like ten minutes, Luis didn't move.

He was still enjoying the rush of excitement – and his foot hurt.

That night, he refused to go to bed. His mother, Sandra, saw him sitting on the sofa well past his bedtime. 'Luis, you should be asleep, you little rascal,' she told him.

'I know, but I played football with Paolo and the big boys today and I don't want the day to be over.'

Sandra smiled. 'But you can go back tomorrow and play again, like your brothers do.'

'Promise?'

'Yes, Luis,' she said gently. She lifted him off the sofa and carried him to the room he shared with his younger brother, Diego. 'You're getting heavy!'

'That's good,' he said, smiling. 'I need to be bigger to win against the older boys.'

Football at the base became part of Luis's routine. As soon as school was over, it was a race against time to get to the pitches and claim one before the other groups got there. Luis's classes finished earlier than those held at the other boys' schools, so he had a head start most days.

On the rare occasions when the weather made
it impossible to play outside, Luis and his brothers
quickly turned to Plan B – playing in the house.
Sandra and Rodolfo gave the boys this freedom, until
Luis accidentally put an end to that by breaking his
parents' bed.

He would never forget his mum's reaction.

'Boys, get in here!'

'What's wrong, Mama?' Luis tried to look
innocent but he knew what was coming.

'How did this happen? There's a crack and the
bed is broken. It wasn't like that this morning, and
I can see dirty footprints. It doesn't take a genius to
know you were playing football in here.'

Luis looked at the floor – partly because he felt
guilty, and partly to look for the footprints that had
given them away. He said nothing, and was relieved
that his brothers didn't put all the blame on him.
After all, it was Paolo who had hit the wild shot. Luis
was just diving to stop the ball breaking other things
in the room.

Sandra shook her head. 'Well, if no-one wants to

answer, you're all banned from going to the pitches for a week.'

The words hung in the air. Luis wanted to protest but he knew from past experience that his mother's decisions on these kinds of things were final. Sandra waved them out of her room, reminding herself that her daughters were far less trouble.

'Thanks for not pointing the finger at me,' he whispered as they headed outside.

'Well, we've got to stick together, but now we're all in trouble,' Paolo replied.

Luis went back to his bedroom and sat on his bed. It was going to be a long week.

CHAPTER 3

THE 'EL CHANGO' EFFECT

Luis loved playing football, but it was hard to keep up with the older boys. One evening, when the whole family had gathered for dinner, he turned to Uncle Sergio – *El Chango* – for answers.

'Uncle, how can I get better? I want to kick the ball harder and score goals like Paolo.'

El Chango grinned. 'You need a good coach. I know just the right person.'

'Who?' Luis said quickly, looking confused.

'Me!'

Luis put down his fork. 'Okay, when can we start?'

Rodolfo shook his head. 'Hold on, Luis. Let's finish

eating first. You can't score goals if you're hungry.'

Luis patiently finished his meal, but he was already thinking about what his uncle would teach him.

The next day, *El Chango* kept his promise. He and Luis walked over to the base early in the morning and found an empty pitch. *El Chango* kicked the ball into the middle of the pitch but held up a hand as Luis turned to chase it. 'Leave it, Luis. We don't need it yet.'

Luis looked at his uncle as if he had two heads. 'What do you mean? How will I get better without a ball?'

'Ah, well that's the first secret. Before you can be a good player, you need to be a clever player. You need to understand the game, the tactics and the tricks.'

Luis sat down. He was willing to listen. After fifteen minutes, *El Chango* decided that the boy had heard enough. 'Okay, now get the ball.'

Luis jumped up. This is more like it, he thought.

'So, what do you want to learn?' *El Chango* asked, palms outstretched.

'I want to be a goalscorer.'

'Okay, show me how you kick the ball. Take a shot over there.'

Luis lined up his shot but the ball just trickled towards the goal.

'Try using this part of your foot instead,' *El Chango* explained, pointing. 'Watch this.'

El Chango dribbled the ball back to the edge of the penalty area, and then fired a shot into the bottom corner.

'Gooooooooooal!' Luis shouted as he ran to get the ball. 'Wow, do it again!'

His uncle grinned. 'No, it's your turn,' he said, patting Luis on the head.

It took some time but, by the end of the morning, Luis was hitting the ball with more accuracy and confidence. He could see the improvement.

'Now let's do some passing. You have to be good at that too.'

'But I just want to be a goalscorer. Other players pass, then I score.'

El Chango shook his head. 'If you want to be a star, you need to practise everything.'

Luis did as he was told. He stood ten paces away from his uncle and they passed the ball back and forth to each other, left foot then right foot.

'Okay, so what time can we come back tomorrow?' Luis asked once they had decided to stop for the day. He was still wiping sweat from his forehead.

'Luis, you've got school tomorrow. I don't want to be in trouble with your mum for helping you skip classes. There's no rush. Keep working on what we practised and we'll come back next weekend.'

The next morning, Sandra woke up to a tapping noise outside. Her first thought was that an animal of some kind was trying to get into the house. She cautiously followed the sound to the front door. When she opened it, there was no sign of any animal. Instead, she found Luis kicking an old ball against the side of the house. He was placing the ball carefully, then reacting quickly to control it as it rebounded back.

'Luis!' she said in the angriest whisper she could manage. 'It's six o'clock. You're crazy. Get back to bed before the neighbours start shouting.'

'Mama, I have to be ready for *El Chango*. I
promised him that I would practise my passing.'

Sandra rolled her eyes and reminded herself to
pinch *El Chango* next time she saw him. 'Luis, if
you want to keep playing, go across the street and
play on the patch over there. But if you fall asleep at
school, there'll be trouble.'

Luis grabbed the ball and crossed to the other side
of the street. That's what he loved about his home
city of Salto. He had the pitches at the army base,
there were lots of big open spaces and it was safe to
play in the streets. It doesn't get any better than this,
he thought, as he kicked the ball high into the air
and ran after it.

But this perfect world was about to be shaken.

CHAPTER 4

ON THE MOVE

'I don't want to move!' Luis screamed, tears running down his cheeks. He made no effort to wipe them away. He heard his parents knocking on his bedroom door, and that just made him scream louder. He wanted to be alone.

Moments earlier, Rodolfo had told his children that they were leaving Salto and moving to Montevideo, the capital city of Uruguay. He had requested a transfer to the army base there. 'This is a new adventure,' he explained. 'Better jobs, better schools and a better life.'

Luis had just stared at his parents in disbelief. 'But … but,' he stammered. The words wouldn't come out. Instead, he ran out of the room and dived onto his bed. He didn't want to cry in front of his dad. How could this be happening?

Eventually, Paolo bravely opened the door and walked over to Luis's bed.

'I said, go away,' Luis yelled without looking up.

'It's me,' his brother said. 'I know it all seems very scary, but let's talk about it.'

Luis relaxed. He was sure that Paolo would be just as angry and maybe they could work together to stop the move. They both had a lot of friends in Salto. He wiped his eyes on his pillow and turned to face his brother.

'What are we going to do?' Luis asked. 'I love Salto. How can they make us leave our friends behind? There must be something we can do to make them change their minds. We could all say that we refuse to go.'

Paolo gave his brother a sympathetic look. 'Luis, the decision has been made. The army has made all the arrangements for Dad, and now we have to support him.'

Luis couldn't believe it. His brother was on their side too. 'I don't want to talk about it anymore. I'm tired. I want to go to sleep and then maybe I'll wake up and find out it was all a nightmare,' Luis said.

Sandra and Rodolfo had expected that Luis would be the most upset about the news, but they had crossed their fingers that the anger would wear off after a few days. Luis had other ideas. He would only say 'Yes' or 'No' when his parents asked him questions and he stormed out of the room as soon as anyone started talking about the move. They knew it was getting out of control.

'What are we going to do about Luis?' Sandra asked her husband. 'I couldn't sleep last night. I hate the thought of him being so unhappy. What if he never accepts that we're leaving Salto?'

'He will, darling. He has to. Once we get there, he'll find new friends quickly. All he needs is a football pitch and he's the happiest boy in the world.'

'I was thinking we could offer him a deal that will make him happier. What if we let him stay in Salto for a few extra weeks, or a month, and then he can join us in Montevideo, once we've set up the house?'

'At this stage, it's worth a try,' Rodolfo agreed. 'Let's speak to him about it after dinner.'

Luis nodded again and again as his parents explained that he could stay with his grandmother for four extra weeks. 'So I can stay with Abuela and I don't need to pack my bag yet?'

'Yes, Luis. If this makes you happy, we'll do it. We'll miss you, but we'll see you soon in Montevideo.'

Luis hugged his mum and raced outside to tell his friends. They would be able to have at least a few more matches on the base after all.

Before he knew it, it was moving day for the rest of the family. As Luis sat on the steps outside the house, he couldn't believe it had arrived so fast. It was all such a blur – the news, the packing, travel plans. Now, there were people everywhere – his dad was carrying suitcases, a man he didn't recognise was loading the suitcases onto a truck, and some of the neighbours were helping to put tape around cardboard boxes.

He had a small bag of clothes ready to take to his

grandmother's house, but all the rest of his clothes and toys were going on the big truck.

Sandra appeared in the doorway. 'Luis, are you sure you packed everything?'

Luis nodded and grinned. 'Don't sell my things before I get there!'

He went in the car with his grandmother to wave to his parents and brothers as they took the bus to Montevideo. They would collect their luggage when they got there. Sandra cried as she waved to Luis.

They would see him in four weeks, but she was sure it would feel like much longer than that. Still, it was a small price to pay to see Luis so much happier. They would get everything ready and then Luis would see just how exciting Montevideo could be. She was already picturing all the fun they would have together.

'Ready for our new life?' Rodolfo asked, hugging his wife. The bus doors closed and the driver started the engine.

'I am,' she said, with a small smile as the bus turned the corner. 'But our new life will only really begin once Luis is with us.'

CHAPTER 5

FINDING HIS FEET IN MONTEVIDEO

Luis made the most of his extra month in Salto, using every spare minute for football. He knew the clock was ticking but he missed his family and it was strange to go to bed each night when they were so far away.

Late one afternoon, Abuela delivered the news: it was time for him to join the family in Montevideo.

This time, there were no tears and no tantrums. Deep down, Luis even felt a little excitement. He packed up his bag and said goodbye to his friends. He wondered if he would ever see them again.

When he arrived in Montevideo, he saw the differences straight away. It was so busy. There were people everywhere.

After a few hours of unpacking and endless stories about their new neighbours, Luis was ready to get outside. 'Paolo, let's take the ball out and play in the street. We can see if the—'

'Hang on, Luis,' Rodolfo interrupted. 'The streets here are too dangerous. We get a lot of cars and they drive fast. It's too risky.'

'Seriously? Okay, well where should we go then?'

Paolo hesitated, then explained: 'There's a park fifteen minutes away. They don't have goalposts but we can take jumpers and make our own.'

'Fifteen minutes? There must be something nearer than that.'

'We're in a big city now,' Rodolfo replied, putting his arm on Luis's shoulder. 'It will take some time but you'll get used to it. Plus, you'll be starting school next week, so you'll be able to play there every day, just like you used to in Salto.'

Luis smiled. That sounded better. He was eager to impress his new classmates after all his practice with *El Chango*.

His first day at school started with a tour of the

building, including a glimpse of the concrete football
pitch. He was introduced to his new teacher who,
in turn, introduced him to the class. He waved shyly
and found a spare seat near the front.

This isn't so bad, he thought. There were a few
pretty girls in his class and he could hear a couple of
the boys talking about football.

At lunchtime, Luis grabbed his sandwich and
rushed out to the football pitch. A group of boys
were already kicking a ball around.

'Who are you?' one of the boys asked, spotting
Luis.

'He's the new kid in our class,' another boy replied.

'My dad is in the army so we moved from Salto,'
Luis explained.

Two of the boys laughed. 'You speak funny!' one
said.

Luis went red. 'This is how I always speak.'

They laughed again, telling him: 'Sorry, we've
already made the teams for today.'

Luis was stunned. Did he really speak differently
from them? No-one had ever told him that before.

And why did they care how many players they had? In Salto, they often had twenty kids on each team.

But he didn't give up. The next day, he got to his classroom a little earlier and put his bag on the chair nearest the door. When the bell sounded at lunchtime, he ran through the corridor and out to the pitch. He was the first one there. 'Now they'll have no choice but to let me play,' he said to himself, grinning.

Soon, the other boys arrived. 'Okay, we've got the new kid,' said Felipe, who seemed to be in charge. He signalled for Luis to come over to their side of the pitch.

'Thanks,' he said.

'We can't lose again today. Nico is unbearable when they win. He's the big guy at the back – he's a really good defender.'

'Don't worry. I'll still score against him,' Luis said, hoping that he could back up this confidence.

Felipe didn't seem convinced. But before he could reply, the game started.

Luis quickly saw that this was a higher level of

football than he was used to. There were lots of good players in Salto, but there were also some who could barely kick the ball. Here, everyone was good.

The first few times Luis got the ball, he tried to be too fancy – a backheel, or too many touches. He saw Felipe glaring at him after one bad pass. I need to stick to what I do best, he reminded himself. Suddenly, Felipe was cutting inside and lining up a shot. Luis sensed there could be a rebound and he raced towards the goal. Sure enough, the goalkeeper fumbled the shot and Luis tapped in the loose ball, just before Nico could block it.

'Yes!' he yelled.

'You might talk funny, but you know how to play,' Felipe said, jumping on Luis's back.

'I told you I'd score against Nico,' Luis said. His goal was one touch from two yards out, but it made all the difference for Luis. By the end of the week, all the boys knew his name.

CHAPTER 6

URRETA FC

When Luis wasn't playing football at school, he was playing at home. As he had told Paolo, if there wasn't a pitch nearby, they would have to make one in the house – and that meant adding to the list of broken items. After a cracked vase, a flattened plant and a dent in the wall, Sandra had seen enough. It was time for the boys to join a team.

But which team? She and Rodolfo asked friends and neighbours for recommendations. When they all suggested the same team, Sandra made the arrangements.

'Luis, get your shoes and some water,' she called. 'You've got a football trial after school. If you do well, you might get to play there every week.'

Luis jumped up and down with excitement. This was amazing news. He was bored of playing against the same boys at school all the time.

'Where, Mama? What team?'

'It's called Urreta FC. They're in the local boys' league, but the season has already started so they may not have room for you.'

The trial was the only thing that Luis could think about all day. This was an opportunity he wanted to take – organised football in safe areas. During his lunch break at school, he was too nervous to eat.

As he stood at the bus stop, waiting with his mum and brother Maximiliano, he wasn't sure what to expect. He had never played in a real game and he was starting to worry that he wouldn't be good enough.

'Luis, you're very quiet,' Sandra said, gently. 'And that usually means that something's bothering you.'

He hesitated. 'I just don't want to make a fool of myself,' he admitted.

'You won't,' she replied. 'You play football all the time. It's just like any other game.'

Once they arrived, Luis forgot all about the nerves. He had never seen such impressive grass pitches and all the boys seemed to have the same kit.

Sandra quickly found Florean Neira, one of the head coaches for Urreta. 'You must be Luis,' Neira said, smiling. 'Welcome to Urreta FC.'

A few of the other boys walked past and Luis waved. He was relieved to see that most of them weren't much bigger than him. A few of them were actually smaller.

'Oh and here's our captain,' Neira said, raising his hand to catch the boy's attention.

'Hi, I'm Gonzalo,' he explained. 'What position do you play?'

'I'm a striker,' Luis replied. 'I love scoring goals.'

'Well, we lost 2–0 in our last game so we need some help. Hopefully, you'll score a lot of goals for us.'

The group of seven-year-olds slowly wandered off to the far side of the pitch, while the older group took the area nearer to the changing room. After a quick warm-up, they started playing three-a-side games.

Luis tried to remember all the things *El Chango* had taught him back in Salto. He never stopped moving, but he always had a plan. He just wanted to get into positions where the other boys could pass the ball to him. 'Nice run,' Neira called.

Every time that a goal was scored, the team that scored it stayed on the pitch, and the team that let it in had to swap with the next team that was waiting. Luis didn't want to come off.

Antonio, one of the skinniest boys in the group, hit a low shot that was going wide until Luis dived in to tap it into the empty goal. He wasn't shy about shouting to his potential new teammates either. 'Lay it back,' he screamed when Antonio ran ahead against the next team. He waited patiently for the pass and then steered the ball into the corner.

After training, Luis drank thirstily from his water bottle. For once, he was tired. 'That was quite a performance,' Neira said, sitting down next to the newcomer. 'You've certainly got an eye for goal. Usually, we like to see players in a few different training sessions but I think we've seen enough

today. We'd like you to join Urreta FC for the rest of
the season.'

'Oh wow, thanks! I can't wait for the first game,'
Luis replied, then realised that he should have
checked with his mum. How would he get to games?
He hadn't thought about that. There wasn't a lot of
money for bus tickets.

They filled out the registration forms and Luis
didn't have to wait long for his first taste of the
action. The next week, Urreta FC were facing one
of their rivals, but Luis was starting on the bench.
He was disappointed, but he understood. 'I'm still
unknown,' he told Paolo. 'But I'll prove myself. I
just need a proper chance.' As the game kicked off,
Luis warmed up along the touchline in his orange
Number 14 shirt. He still had a one peso coin in his
hand ready for his bus ticket home and he tucked
it into his sock to keep it safe. Maybe it would be a
lucky charm, he thought.

While he waited for a chance to shine, Luis
watched the opposition defenders closely. One was
slow and didn't seem to understand his position. He

also watched his new teammates to learn their styles. When would they look for a long pass? What was the sign that they would cross the ball?'

With Urreta FC losing 2–0, Neira turned to Luis. 'Okay, let's see what the new boy can do. Luis, you're coming on to play as a second striker. Get yourself in the box whenever you can.'

Luis threw off his tracksuit and ran onto the field. The grass felt amazing. He was still learning the game, but he definitely understood how to out-think others in the box.

He quickly found the slow defender and stayed close to him. He knew he would be able to outsprint him easily. Gonzalo's long punt gave Luis his first sight of goal. 'See ya,' he shouted as he raced ahead of the defender. He got to the ball before the goalkeeper, took it round him and calmly knocked it into the net.

'What's your name?' he asked the slow defender as the game restarted.

'Marco.'

'Can I call you Slow-mo?' Luis asked, sneering at

Marco. Ever since he had begun playing on the army base, he had enjoyed arguing and causing trouble on the pitch.

Slow-mo was caught out again two minutes later. Antonio's shot was blocked but the ball bounced loose in the box. Luis was the quickest to react and he poked the ball through the goalkeeper's legs.

At 2–2, Urreta pushed for the win – and Luis was still fresh. He had only been on for fifteen minutes. Again, he had Slow-mo in his sights.

'Come on, give me a break!' Slow-mo complained when Luis appeared next to him. The next time the ball came forward, he pushed Luis to the floor but the referee didn't give a free-kick.

'Can I call you Wimp?' Marco asked, grinning.

This just made Luis angry and more determined to win the game for his team. With time running out, he scored again. He had always dreamt of scoring a match-winning goal – usually it was an unstoppable volley or a diving header. But in his Urreta FC debut, he settled for a tap-in.

His was the only orange shirt in the box when

a left-winger named Miguel lobbed the ball across, but Luis judged the bounce perfectly. The goalkeeper missed the ball and Luis touched it over the line.

It didn't matter that he was the new boy or that most of his teammates still didn't know his name; they were calling him 'El Salta', a name that would stick with him throughout his career. When he slid to his knees to celebrate, they all dived on him.

'I've always said that I know a great player when I see one,' Neira said, puffing out his chest proudly. 'A hat-trick in thirty minutes is brilliant, but I bet he could score even more in a full game.'

After the game, Luis was at the centre of everything, telling jokes and laughing at his teammates' impressions of his goal celebration. 'Just wait, I'll have a better celebration ready for the next game,' he told them.

As Luis walked back to the bus stop that night, he had a huge grin on his face. He had talked and talked about wanting to be a goalscorer. Now, he actually was one.

CHAPTER 7

HIGHS AND LOWS

On the pitch, everything was going smoothly for Luis. But off the pitch, it was a different story.

'Luis, I need to talk to you,' Sandra said very seriously one day when Luis got home from school. 'Come and sit down.'

'Can it wait until after football? I promised to meet my friends.'

'No, it needs to be now,' his mum replied firmly.

Luis threw down his bag in frustration but then turned to see tears in his mum's eyes.

'Mama, what's wrong?' he asked. But he could guess – he had heard his parents arguing every night for the past month. He knew it wasn't a coincidence

46

that his grandmother had moved to Montevideo to help look after Luis and his younger brothers Maximiliano and Diego.

'Sit down, darling,' she said, her voice suddenly very weak. 'There's no easy way to say this. Your dad has moved out. He got a job in Carrasco and is going to live there. You'll still see him, of course. He wants you to know that. But it means that things are going to change around here. I'm going to start working in the evenings and I'm going to need your help here. Maximiliano and Diego look up to you, please keep an eye on them.'

Luis just kept nodding to everything. He still had a lot of questions. Was this permanent? Would they be able to pay the bills? But his mum looked so tired. He just stood up and hugged her. Sandra couldn't hold back the tears. She sobbed as Luis tried to console her.

As Luis lay on his bed that night, he replayed the conversation over and over. He was angry, but he wasn't sure who he was angry with. He just wished that things didn't have to change.

But he never complained, despite sharing a tiny room with Maximiliano and Diego and surviving on the cheapest food available. Football was his escape. More specifically, he had fallen in love with the local team, Nacional. He continued to impress at Urreta FC and wasn't afraid to tell Felipe, Nico and all the other boys at school that he would one day wear the Nacional shirt as their star striker.

When Urreta FC began training at Nacional's home stadium, the Gran Parque Central, Luis couldn't believe it. He was running on the same grass as his heroes. Neira knew this would give his team all the motivation they needed. 'You never know who's watching,' he told them at the start of every training session.

At night, Luis dreamt of meeting the Nacional players and being invited to join the team. 'It's going to happen, Abuela,' he said one night as they ate a plate of rice.

'You have to keep improving, though,' she told her grandson. 'As soon as you stand still, other boys will catch you up.'

Towards the end of the next season, Luis felt
a tap on his shoulder. He turned to see Neira, his
coach, grinning. 'I wanted to be the one to tell you.
A Nacional scout has been watching you here for
the last three weeks. They want you to start training
with their youth team.'

Luis's legs turned to jelly and his head was
spinning. 'Me? Really? Coach, if this is one of your
jokes, it's too cruel.'

'I know how much you love Nacional. Do you
really think I'd joke about this?'

Luis relaxed. 'That's true.' He was already
picturing himself wearing the Number 9 shirt.

'Their youth scout is going to call your mum this
week to make all the arrangements. They'll give you
some money to cover the travel costs as well. But I
made them promise that I could be the one to tell
you the good news!'

Luis punched the air. He couldn't wait to tell his
friends. For once, he was up early to get ready for
school. He wanted to be there before the first class
so he could give Felipe and Nico the news. 'Just

remember us when you're rich and famous,' Felipe said as he gave Luis a high five.

There was still a long way to go but now whenever Luis dreamt of becoming a professional footballer, the images felt just a little bit clearer.

CHAPTER 8

FINDING HIS WAY AT NACIONAL

Wilson Píriz looked across at the boy in the doorway and waved him into the room. 'Hi, Luis,' he said. 'I'm Wilson and I'll be your club representative throughout your time with Nacional. My door is always open. If you have any questions, you can always come to me.'

Luis grinned. Wait until the other boys hear that I have a Nacional representative, he thought.

He only saw Wilson occasionally during his first few seasons training at Nacional, but Wilson was keeping a close eye on the young goalscorer. Even within his first few months at the club, Luis had become a major topic of conversation for the coaches.

'He's clumsy and his control is bad,' one coach claimed. 'He's a good kid but I'm not sure he's going to get any better. Good defenders will stop him easily.'

'But he scores goals – that's what I care about,' another replied. 'And we *have* good defenders here. Luis still scores against them.'

'Think about it. How much of it is skill and how much is luck? He always seems to get lucky bounces and most of his goals are tap-ins. Have you seen him shoot from outside the penalty area? I'm not saying that we shouldn't keep him, but I think we have to be realistic about how far he can go.'

'He's a magnet for the ball in the penalty area, though. We have other players that can shoot from twenty yards, but how many teams have a striker who always knows where the ball will bounce in the box? That's a skill. It's a striker's instinct.'

Back and forth they went – to the point where Wilson felt that every training session sparked the debate. He tried not to be dragged into the conversation but, when he had to give an opinion, he was clear. 'That boy is going to be a star. We can work on his technique, but he has two qualities that are much harder to coach: he's a hard worker and he's a goalscorer.'

Luis was unaware of all this discussion. He was just happy to be playing for Nacional. He spent long afternoons and nights there, doing extra running, as well as eating a free meal at the club canteen. His permanent smile was always impossible for Yudith, the cook, to resist. He knew a few of the other players from his time at Urreta FC, including two of his good friends, Víctor and Martin. All this made Nacional feel like a second home.

'Swing some crosses in,' Luis called to Víctor one morning after training. He was never in a hurry to leave once the session was over.

'I'm going to mark you,' Martin said, smiling. 'I want to see how you always manage to create space and get into the perfect position to score.'

'Challenge accepted.'

Luis had a whole list of different tricks he liked to use. As the first cross came in, he quickly judged where the ball would land and used a little nudge to get to the ball before Martin.

'Foul!' Martin protested, as if a referee might suddenly appear and blow the whistle.

'A referee wouldn't have given that and you know it!' Luis shot back.

A crowd of other players was gathering behind the goal, curious to watch the action. Santiago, the team's goalkeeper, was now standing between the posts, giving Luis more of a test.

Victor tried another cross. It flew too close to Santiago, but the goalkeeper fumbled the catch. Luis pounced on the rebound. 'Thanks very much,' he shouted. He was enjoying this.

'How did it land right at your feet?' Santiago moaned. 'You're so lucky.'

'Some call it luck, some call it skill,' Luis replied, laughing.

Martin shrugged, then smiled. 'Okay, maybe I was wrong. As long as you keep scoring and we keep winning, you can call it whatever you want.'

Surrounded by good players, Luis just had to

provide the finishing touch. My job is easy, he thought. But just to be sure that he had luck on his side, he kept slotting the lucky peso coin into his sock for every game. Despite all his confidence in front of his teammates, he sometimes worried that his luck would run out.

CHAPTER 9

THE ULTIMATUM

Luis had impressed everyone with the way he juggled his football with his schoolwork and the extra responsibilities at home. But then the problems started. For the first time since joining Paolo's friends at the army base, football didn't seem to have the answers. It didn't take long for Sandra to notice.

'How was training last night?' she asked one morning.

'Fine,' he grunted back, opening a bag of crisps that Yudith had given him for the walk home.

'Luis, you've been eating more junk food than ever recently. At least have something healthier. You won't be able to move on the pitch!'

'Whatever. I'm going to a party at Nico's house tonight so I won't be here for dinner.'

Sandra frowned. 'You've got a game tomorrow morning. If you go to that party, you'll be tired for the game. Your teammates are counting on you. I won't stop you, but just think about the consequences.'

Luis rolled his eyes. Didn't she realise that he could do both? Even though his team had lost their last three games, and he hadn't scored in any of the losses, he felt he was still playing well.

But he wasn't fooling Wilson. He was still one of Luis's biggest fans within the club, but he found himself having to defend him on a regular basis.

'He's a disgrace and he needs to go,' one of the head coaches argued. 'Last week we received a complaint that he shouted at a stranger, then squirted water at him. Is that the kind of player we want representing Nacional? He clearly doesn't care anymore, and there are hundreds of boys who would love the chance to take his place.'

Wilson's shoulders sagged. How many chances did Luis want? 'Let me talk to him. If you don't see signs of improvement within the next month, then you can make your decision.'

With that timing agreed, Wilson called Luis to his office.

'Hey, Wilson. What can I do for you?' Luis said, cockily. He looked tired and his hair was scruffy.

'Come in and sit down,' Wilson said firmly. He was still furious about the stories he had heard.

'Okay, okay. No need to get angry,' Luis replied with a big grin.

'Let me ask you a question: Do you want a better life, with a big house and a flashy car? Or would you prefer to live on the street or end up in jail?'

Luis's grin disappeared.

'That's the crossroads you're at, Luis. You go to parties, you hang around with friends who smoke, suddenly you care more about girls than football, and you can't be bothered in training because you're tired from the night before. You don't eat the right food, even though we've got the canteen upstairs giving you free food. Then to make matters worse, even when you're playing football, you embarrass the club with bad behaviour. I believe in you, I've fought for you, and I want you to be successful. I also know that life at home isn't easy for you. But you're one mistake away from being kicked out – do you understand? That's the club's ultimatum – sort yourself out or get out.'

Luis had listened to everything in silence. By the end, he was staring at the ground, with tears forming in his eyes. 'I'm sorry, Wilson. I can do better.'

'Luis, we need more than just words. Prove it. Show us that football is a top priority. Be professional, turn up on time and put in the work. This is a second chance that many players wouldn't get. Don't waste it.'

Luis got up to leave the room but stopped at the door and turned around. 'Wilson, thank you for not giving up on me.'

And then he headed for the pitch. It was time to make things right. Wilson had always treated him like family and he hated letting him down. The best way to show that he was sorry was by giving his all on the pitch.

'After all this, if I do make it to the top, I probably should buy Wilson a car too,' he said to himself.

CHAPTER 10

SOFI

Despite all the warnings from Wilson, Luis needed a break. He had worked hard to regain the faith of the coaches at Nacional and he was scoring goals again. The party that evening at Fabric nightclub was the perfect reward. It also changed his life.

He met up with his friends at Nico's house first and then the group headed for Fabric. Image was everything and they didn't want to arrive too early. They huddled at a table to watch the girls arrive and discuss the ones that caught their eyes. There was no game the next day for the Nacional youth team, so Luis didn't feel so guilty about being there.

When he went to order a drink, a tall guy

appeared next to him in the queue and said: 'Luis, right?'

Luis hesitated. Was this some kind of trap set up by Nacional? He couldn't really lie, so he nodded.

'Don't look so suspicious. I played against you when you were at Urreta FC. I was in goal; you scored a hat-trick. I'm Kiko.'

Luis shook his hand. He didn't remember the goalkeeper, but then he had scored a lot of hat-tricks for Urreta FC.

'Sorry, I guess.' He wasn't sure what else to say.

'I was a terrible keeper anyway,' Kiko said, laughing. 'I'm here with my girlfriend, her sister and their friends. I'm kind of outnumbered. Bring your drink over and I'll introduce you.'

Before Luis could say no, he was being guided over to their table. 'I'm just catching up with a friend,' he called to Felipe as he walked by. 'Keep my seat, I'll be back in five minutes.'

But that plan went out of the window as soon as he met Sofia. 'Luis, this is my girlfriend's sister, Sofia, but everyone calls her Sofi.'

Luis was speechless. Sofi was beautiful. He was usually good with jokes but suddenly he didn't know what to say.

Kiko filled the silence. 'I played against Luis a few years ago. Now he plays for Nacional.'

'Well, I'll have to come to see one of your games then. But if I do, I expect you to score an extra goal just for me.' She winked at Luis, and he grinned.

'You've got a deal.'

They talked a little, danced a little and made plans to meet up the next day. When Luis finally found Felipe and Nico at the end of the night, they were shaking their heads.

'What?' he asked.

'How do you do it?' Nico asked, laughing. 'Even with those rabbit teeth, the prettiest girls want to dance with you.'

Luis shrugged innocently. 'I can't help it if I'm charming.'

The more time Luis spent with Sofi, the more he liked her, but when Wilson heard that Luis had a girlfriend, he feared the worst. After all the work to save his Nacional career, maybe he was heading in the wrong direction again.

But the opposite happened. Sofi quickly proved to be a good influence. She didn't just show up at his games, she encouraged him to try harder in training and to take school more seriously. Life at home was still difficult for Luis, but Sofi made everything better.

Before one of Luis's games, Wilson walked along the touchline to provide some final words of encouragement. Luis was doing the last few stretches of his warm-up and he waved at his good friend.

'El Salta, I see that Sofi is here,' Wilson called. 'How about this: if you score today, I'll give you a few extra pesos so you can take her out for dinner.'

Luis's eyes lit up. He forgot all about the stretches and put his arm round Wilson. 'You might as well put that money aside now. I'll come to collect it after the game.'

He earned his little bonus within ten minutes. One defender slipped and Luis was through on goal. The angle was tight and another defender was racing across. Luis didn't panic. He faked a shot, knocked the ball through the defender's legs and curled the ball into the far corner. He ran to the touchline, blew a kiss to Sofi and then pointed over to Wilson, just in case he had forgotten the agreement.

After the game, Wilson handed an envelope to Luis. 'I keep my promises, Luis. Great goal.' As he walked away towards his car, Wilson turned and added: 'Hang on to Sofi. She's good for you.'

CHAPTER 11

GOAL MACHINE

With every passing week, Luis felt a little closer to his dream of playing for the Nacional first team. He won the top goalscorer award for the youth league and was presented with the trophy by Rubén Sosa, one of his heroes.

Luis was starting to watch more football too, whether it was at a friend's house or a local bar. He saw games from the local Uruguayan leagues and sometimes other parts of South America or even Europe. That's when he first discovered Gabriel Batistuta, the deadly striker from Argentina. Luis was a different type of player – smaller, quicker, not as powerful – but he loved Batistuta's passion and his ability to score from any angle.

It was inspiring. Luis dominated the Under 15s league, scoring twenty-five goals that season. He was unstoppable in the Under 16s squad too. Now he wanted to set a more challenging target. 'Okay, aim for fifty goals,' Maximiliano said at dinner one night. Everyone laughed, except Luis.

'I accept the challenge,' he said, putting on a funny voice and offering to shake his brother's hand.

That summer, he trained harder than ever, with Sofi joining him whenever she could. Two seasons ago, he had started on the bench. He never wanted that to happen again.

Luis saved his best for a game against Huracán del Paso de la Arena. Even during the warm-up, he could tell he was going to have a good game. After two minutes, he scored with a low shot from the edge of the box. Five minutes later, he got another with a header after the goalkeeper missed a cross. By half-time, he had scored seven goals.

'Ease up, Luis,' his manager said, grinning. 'Don't you feel bad for their keeper?'

'I want more,' Luis said, with a serious expression. 'I've never got ten before. Please don't take me off.'

His manager wouldn't have dared. He knew what kind of meltdown that would have caused.

From the kick-off, Victor and Martin passed their way through the defence. Martin hit a powerful shot that bounced back off the post. Who was following in for a tap-in? Luis, of course. He held up his right hand and three fingers on his left hand. Now, he had scored eight goals.

He finished the game with eleven goals. By then, even Luis felt a little guilty. One of the defenders was crying and some of the parents were yelling.

'Some days, it just feels like I'll score every time I get the ball, or I just know where the ball is going to be and I can always get there first,' he told Victor in the changing room afterwards. 'Today was one of those days.'

Even during such an impressive season, Luis couldn't quite stay out of trouble. Wilson had plenty of sources and was always the first to know when 'El

Salta' stepped out of line. The day after a 3–0 victory, he called Luis into his office.

'Luis, tell me about yesterday's game,' he began.

'It was good. We won. That's about it.'

'Ah okay, so I must be confused then, because I heard that you had a tantrum and stormed off after the game.'

Luis looking at the ceiling. 'I know, it's bad. I was just frustrated that I didn't score. The team winning is the most important thing but I'm a striker. It's my job to score, and I didn't.'

'But Luis, you need to lead by example. You can't score in every game. Even Batistuta can't. Your temper gets you into trouble and it's only going to get worse in the older teams. They'll know about your reputation and defenders will try every trick to make you snap.'

'I'll change. I'll be calmer. Sometimes I just want to win so much that I forget about everything else. I forget about how I'm supposed to behave and I just go on instinct.'

Wilson nodded. 'I can't be angry at you for

wanting to win. That's a great quality to have. But I want you to work harder at staying under control. Otherwise, you'll let your teammates down.'

Luis was soon scoring again and these kinds of incidents were quickly forgotten. He finished the season with sixty-three goals and a growing fan club. 'I doubt you'll have much time for me soon,' Sofi joked. 'There will be so many autographs to sign.'

'As long as you're still my number-one fan, I'll be happy,' said Luis. 'I keep telling you, you're my lucky charm. Every game you come to, I score.'

Over at the Nacional offices, Wilson had a little extra spring in his step these days. He had fought for Luis to stay at Nacional, and now he looked like a genius. Luis was a regular topic of conversation all summer at the club. All the coaches knew that Luis could be a handful, but his talent as a goalscorer was clear. It would soon be time to promote him to the first team and see just how good he could become.

CHAPTER 12

HEARTBREAK

Luis had been making plans all day – a walk in the park, a picnic, maybe some live music in the main square. But when the café door opened and Sofi walked in with a sad look on her face, he knew instantly that those plans were going to change. She could barely look him in the eye. Every time she did, tears flickered and she looked away.

'What is it?' Luis asked, hugging her. 'What's wrong?'

Sofi wanted to explain everything, but all she could manage was: 'I'm so sorry. I can't believe this is happening.'

Luis's heart skipped a beat. Was she dumping him? But that wasn't it at all.

Sofi finally broke the news. 'Luis, my dad was offered a job in Spain. Business is bad here so we're moving to Barcelona. I don't know what else to say. I have to go with him. We're leaving in three weeks.'

With the words finally out, she burst into tears.

Luis wanted to cry too. Just when everything seemed to be perfect, his world was being turned upside down again. Her family had welcomed Luis into their house and they thought his cheekiness was charming. Whenever he pictured his future, they were all in it. Was this really goodbye? Luis didn't know the price of a flight to Barcelona, but he knew he didn't have that kind of money.

They just walked aimlessly, holding hands but saying nothing. Both were lost in their own thoughts, trying to imagine what life would be like once they were torn apart.

Finally, Luis broke the silence. 'We still have today. No-one can take that away from us.'

Sofi nodded. 'You're right. Let's make the most of it. Everything else can wait.'

They headed for the park and Luis unwrapped two sandwiches which he had picked up from the Nacional canteen. They sat close together and watched the people passing by. Luis loved to make Sofi laugh by making up stories about the passers-by. Even now, with a broken heart, he gave it his all.

'You see the old man over there,' he said, pointing. 'He seems happy but he has just remembered that he forgot to put on his pants. And that lady on the bench is pretending to read the newspaper but really she's forgotten her glasses.'

Sofi giggled. 'I'm going to miss these games,' she said quietly.

The next three weeks passed painfully quickly. When the day that Luis was dreading arrived, he insisted on going to the airport with Sofi, even if it would make the goodbye even harder.

'Remember our promise,' she said, giving him one last kiss and taking out her passport. 'We will call and email whenever we can. We won't give up.'

Luis nodded. 'If we are meant to be together, we will find a way.'

He waved and waved until she was out of sight. Then he fell to the floor and sobbed, as travellers did their best to wheel their cases around him.

Luis spent the next few days feeling sorry for himself. He stayed in bed, skipped training and yelled at anyone who dared to disturb him.

Finally, Sandra couldn't take it anymore. 'Luis, enough is enough,' she told him. 'We all love Sofi and I know it hurts at the moment. But you can use these emotions to take your football to the next level. Use this anger to train harder, score more goals and earn the money to visit Sofi. Could there be any bigger motivation for you to become a star?'

Luis thought about it. His mum was right. Instead of crying into his pillow, he should be out there running extra laps and lifting weights. He wanted to become a professional footballer – he already knew that – but now he felt that he *had* to become a professional. His future with Sofi depended on it.

CHAPTER 13

OVERCOMING THE BOOS

With football as his number-one focus, Luis was
unstoppable. The Nacional coaches were talking
about Luis for all the right reasons now, saying: 'He
still has weaknesses, but I've never seen anyone with
those instincts in the penalty area. He scores from
any angle. He's not the quickest or the most skilful
but he's so clever and he never gets tired.'

'So what are we waiting for? He dominated the
youth leagues, let's see what he can do against the
big boys. He should be training with the first team.'

Just like that, Luis's dream came true. He was
following in his heroes' footsteps and he couldn't
help but imagine where his career might go next.

But there was nothing easy about taking that step up to the first team. The luck and deadly finishing that had been part of his game for the past few years had deserted him. Luis had already started to prepare himself for the possibility of being dropped down to the reserves. It was hard to prepare for games with all these thoughts running through his head. He just wished that Sofi was there – she always knew the right thing to say.

Luckily, he could rely on the support of his family. 'The fans are crazy to doubt you,' Paolo said. 'One minute they love you, the next they hate you.'

'I guess that's part of the deal as a footballer,' Luis replied. 'I'm more determined than ever to start taking my chances and scoring goals. They can doubt me as much as they want, that just fires me up.'

'Well, we'll be there to cheer you on. Wilson dropped off some tickets for us.'

That afternoon, the fans piled into the Gran Parque Central. The stadium announcer was reading out the teams: 'Number 9, Luis Suárez.'

'Booooooooooo!' The crowd's opinion was loud

and clear. His own fans were turning on him.

Luis took a deep breath. It had been like this for a month now. He would do everything right, get into the perfect position, then fluff his shot. 'Donkey! Wooden leg!' the fans screamed. Luis had grown up in Montevideo from the age of seven. He was one of their own. It didn't seem to matter.

His manager, Martín Lasarte, had backed him in every interview. Now Lasarte was on the touchline, waving for Luis to run over for some final instructions. 'Listen, I don't understand why the fans are acting this way, but don't pay attention to it. You've been playing well. Once you score a couple of goals, everything will change. Keep your head up.'

Luis worked harder than ever that afternoon, chasing every ball and dribbling past defenders, even with his own fans jeering. Then, in the second half, he shut them up with a wonder goal. Luis received a pass with his back to goal and swivelled past his defender. He heard teammates calling for a pass, but the ball was sitting up perfectly for a half volley. He trusted his instincts and whipped a shot towards goal. From the moment it left his foot, he knew he had done something special. The ball curved past the goalkeeper's outstretched hand and into the net.

The stadium erupted. Paolo and Maximiliano were jumping up and down with all the other Nacional fans. Luis's teammates knew what that goal meant to him. They followed him over to the corner flag to celebrate. 'Finally!' Luis yelled, kissing the Nacional badge on his shirt. 'Finally!'

From that day on, there were no more boos. 'I told you all,' Lasarte said, grinning at the reporters. 'That kid is a special talent. Today, you saw him take the next step towards being a huge star. He is going to score many more goals for Nacional. You'll be sorry that you ever doubted him.'

As Luis had predicted, he just needed that first goal. He scored eleven more over the rest of the 2005/06 season, helping Nacional win the Uruguayan league. 'A few months ago, I was a nobody. Now I'm a champion,' he told his teammates as they sprayed champagne in the dressing room. 'It doesn't get any better than this!'

Luis was picturing what it would be like to become one of the all-time greats at Nacional – the kind of player that the fans would talk about for years and years. He had improved so much in just one season with the first team, and he had plenty more tricks up his sleeve.

But when he met with his agent, Daniel Fonseca, the following week, he found out that it wasn't just people in Uruguay who had been keeping an eye on him that season. It became clear that Luis had become a hot property.

CHAPTER 14

HEADING FOR EUROPE

As soon as Luis heard the rumours, his mind was racing. Two clubs were interested in signing him, if Nacional were willing to sell. Suddenly, he didn't know where he would be playing for the 2006/07 season.

His agent, Daniel, called later that afternoon. 'Luis, nothing is definite yet, but we need to be prepared. You know about Flamengo in the Brazilian league, but what about Anderlecht? That's in Belgium, so you would have to be willing to move to Europe.'

'I want to play at the next level so it seems like both are good options. When will we know more?'

'I'm expecting a call within the next few days and then we'll have to give our answer quickly.'

'Which do you think is—?'

'Sorry, Luis. I have to answer another call that I've been waiting for. Hold that thought and we'll speak again later, I promise. In the meantime, think things over – and enjoy it. This is an exciting time for you.'

But Luis needed to know more. He went outside and started walking, with no real plan. The European option of Anderlecht sounded good if it meant that he was closer to Sofi. But how close? That's what he wanted to know.

After almost an hour of walking, he found himself near the National Library of Uruguay. He had only ever been inside once, but maybe he would find his answers there. He rushed inside to find a map. He pulled a thick book off the shelf and ran over to a small desk in the corner.

He found Belgium and traced a line down to Spain with his finger. It didn't look that far.

When in doubt, there was always one person that Luis could turn to – Wilson.

'Hmmm, well the first thing I should tell you is not to be distracted by these stories,' Wilson said. 'You still play for Nacional and you need to give your all for the club. But here's what I know. It would take a long time in the car, that's for sure. It's further than it looks. Taking the plane won't be cheap but it's quick – maybe two or three hours.'

Luis liked the sound of that. But what did he really know about the Belgian league? He hadn't heard of Anderlecht until earlier that week and he couldn't name a single other team in that country. When he spoke to Daniel later, he got the sense that his agent was equally unsure about the move to Anderlecht. They agreed to be patient and wait for the right offer.

While Luis tried to block out the rumours and focus on Nacional, a third option was quietly developing. Groningen, from the Dutch league, had sent Grads Fühler and Hans Nijland to Montevideo to watch Nacional in action a few weeks earlier. They did not have Luis on their scouting list, but he stole the show with two goals and a tireless all-round performance.

The scouts had some re-thinking to do. 'This could be our lucky night,' Grads said. 'We might have accidentally found the next big star. Suárez was incredible and he's still so young. He'd be an instant success in a Groningen shirt.'

'He fits everything we need,' agreed Hans. 'I think we need to focus on Suárez. That's going to be my feedback.'

'But we need to move quickly,' Grads replied. 'He won't be a hidden gem for long if he keeps playing like this.' By the end of the month, Groningen had made their bid.

'I've never heard of them,' Luis admitted, when Daniel explained that Groningen had joined the chase. 'Is this really a step forward?'

'The Dutch league is strong,' Daniel explained. 'Ajax, Feyernoord and PSV are always good and it could be a short stop on the way to one of the bigger European teams. Trust me, Barcelona, Real Madrid and Manchester United all keep a close eye on the brightest stars in the Dutch league.'

It would be near to Sofi too, Luis thought.

Daniel read his mind. 'I know what you're thinking and I've already checked.'

'Checked what?'

'Two hours and two minutes. That's the flight time to Barcelona.'

Luis smiled. His agent knew him well. 'I think this is it, Daniel. It feels right.'

'Okay, let me speak to Nacional. They've only just received Groningen's bid but I can let them know that you're interested.'

All Luis could do was sit back and wait. But waiting wasn't one of his strengths. To pass the time, he dribbled a ball around the house and practised balancing it on the back of his neck. He didn't want to tell anyone else about it yet – not until he knew if it was a real possibility. But how would his family react? He imagined they would probably cry about the thought of him being alone in Holland, but they would be happy that he was following his dream.

Daniel called to say that there would be no decision for at least another two days and that Luis should report for training as usual the next morning.

That felt strange. It felt unfair to his teammates to just turn up as if nothing was happening.

Then he had to fly to Holland for the medical test. When the deal was finally completed, Luis celebrated with a can of Coke. He called Sofi that afternoon and they both cried tears of joy.

Luis had packed two suitcases for the trip and began settling into his temporary hotel room. Groningen gave him a couple of days off to get used to life in Holland, and Luis took the chance to fly to Barcelona to see Sofi.

After two special days in Barcelona, Sofi went to the airport to wave Luis off as he returned to Holland. But he couldn't face another goodbye. Suddenly, he had an idea.

'Come with me!' he blurted out. 'Let's live together in Holland as a proper couple. I can't be apart from you again.'

Sofi was stunned. She was the sensible one – the one who thought everything through before making decisions. But every bone in her body was telling her to go with Luis. There were so many unanswered questions but she didn't care. 'Let's do it,' she said, shaking with excitement. 'I have to tell my parents first, though. We need their blessing.'

Luis nodded and waited nervously as Sofi dialled the number. He heard her explain to her father that she wanted to spend some time in Holland. Luis watched Sofi's face, trying to guess what the response was. Then he saw a big smile break out and Sofi gave the thumbs up. 'Holland here we come!' he screamed, hugging Sofi and lifting her off the ground.

By the time they landed in Groningen, though, some of their worries started to sink in. They were in a new city, where they knew no-one. 'That's all part of the adventure,' Luis whispered as they waited for a taxi. 'Plus, Bruno Silva plays for Groningen. He's Uruguayan too.'

What a difference two years made! After waving goodbye to Sofi in Montevideo and thinking he might never see her again, destiny had brought them back together. As he prepared to join his new Groningen teammates, he couldn't stop smiling.

CHAPTER 15

DIETS AND DIVING

'Slow down, Luis!' Bruno shouted. 'You're going to crash. Is this how you thank me for teaching you to drive?'

Luis tapped the brake and grinned at his friend. 'Come on, old man. Where's your sense of adventure?'

Bruno shook his head. 'Ever since you signed for Groningen, I've been getting grey hairs. It's no coincidence.'

Luis had faced worries of his own. The start to his time in Holland had been harder than he had expected, even with Sofi by his side. Bruno had been the perfect guide, but Luis was trying to learn a new language, adjust to a new city and get used to new teammates all at once. Plus, he couldn't rely on his mum to make his bed! He and Sofi had bought bikes to explore the city, but now he was enjoying the freedom of having a car.

'How's the diet going?' Bruno asked, hoping to wind Luis up.

His efforts succeeded. 'What? Who told you about that?' Luis shot back angrily.

'Eyes on the road, Luis.'

'The diet is embarrassing enough without you spreading it around. Keep it to yourself. I'm doing what they say, but who wants to drink water all day? Sometimes I just need a Coke and a pizza.'

'Whatever, Fatty,' Bruno replied, and Luis swung a playful punch at him.

'To be honest, I'm not sure it's making a difference,' Luis said. 'I'm still playing with the reserves and they don't trust me. I haven't been given a fair chance to prove myself.'

'Look, here's some free advice. As I've told you many times...'

'I know – Holland isn't Uruguay, blah blah blah. I get it.'

'Let me finish,' Bruno said, holding up his palm. 'You think you've heard it a million times – well, why aren't you listening? If you keep ignoring the coach and arguing with referees, you'll never play for the first team. The manager has told me that. No diving, no faking.'

'If a defender touches me in the box, I'm going to try to win the penalty,' said Luis. 'What's wrong with that?'

'But when you try to trick the referees, you get a reputation. Then they won't even give you the obvious penalties.'

'Look, just tell the manager that if he gives me the central striker role, I'll prove myself. That's all it will take.'

Luis stopped at the traffic lights and picked up his thermos of *mate*, a Uruguayan specialty.

Bruno shook his head. 'It would help if you didn't bring that flask to training every day too. You look like you're going to a picnic.'

Luis laughed. 'It sounds like you're more Dutch than Uruguayan now, Bruno!'

Just like at Nacional, the coaches were divided on Luis's potential. Some feared that the new signing was going to be a big flop, and they jumped around furiously when he dived to the floor without being touched. 'Get up!' they screamed, waving their arms.

And Luis did not always make the most of the chances he got. Manager Ron Jans tapped him on the shoulder one morning after training. 'Luis, we're going to change things for the next game. You're going to be starting up front. We need goals so get on the last defender and look for the long ball over the top.'

Luis was desperate to score. Even in the pouring rain, he sprinted after every ball, but the passes were always too high and too long. He waved his arms to encourage his teammates to keep it simple. With Groningen struggling, Ron signalled for a substitution. Luis looked over at the electronic board and saw his number. His head dropped as he walked slowly to the touchline, then straight to the dugout.

Suddenly, he heard shouting. He looked up to see

Ron pointing at him, yelling, 'Don't sit there sulking. Show some respect.' As Ron's face got redder and redder, he threw his umbrella to the floor and part of it snapped off.

Luis was in total shock. He didn't know what to say. He looked at Bruno, who was sitting at the other end of the dugout. 'I was disappointed to come off but I didn't mean to offend him,' he called. 'Why is he so angry?'

Bruno walked over and put a hand on Luis's shoulder. 'In Holland, all the players shake the manager's hand when they come off. It is expected – even if you are unhappy. Don't worry. I'll explain that you didn't know about that.'

Luis stood by Bruno's side after the game as he told Ron about the misunderstanding. Ron listened, nodded and gave his answer. He patted Luis on the shoulder and walked off to speak to the reporters.

'Tell me, tell me, what did he say?' Luis asked Bruno impatiently.

'He knows it was an innocent mistake. He said you'll get another chance.'

Ron kept his promise and gave Luis another
chance in the starting line-up against Vitesse. This
was a make-or-break opportunity. 'One more bad
game and I might be sold,' he told Bruno as they
parked at the training ground.

Luis barely slept the night before the game. This
was his chance to prove himself to the manager and
the fans. But things got off to a bad start. Groningen
fell 3–1 behind and Luis could imagine the headlines.
Somehow, he would get the blame. So he took charge
of the situation. With ten minutes to go, he won a
penalty, then in the closing minutes he equalised with
a clinical finish. 'We can still win this,' he screamed.

With only a minute to go, no-one really believed
him. But Luis was serious. He won the ball back
straightaway, dribbled past three defenders and
fired an unstoppable shot into the top corner. His
teammates watched with stunned faces for a second,
then chased him towards the corner flag.

This rescue act made all the difference. Suddenly,
fans were spotting him around the city and asking for
autographs. His days in the reserves were over.

'Everything was worth it for a day like today,' he told Bruno in the dressing room after the game. 'The fans were singing my name.'

'I always knew you'd prove yourself, El Salta. Now you've got to keep it going. I guess you've earned a Coke and a pizza tonight, though.'

Luis was now a favourite with the fans and he was determined to prove that the Vitesse game was no fluke. He finished the season with ten goals, but knew he could do much better. His partnership with Erik Nevland was one of the best in the league and, with a full preseason to work with his teammates, he was setting his sights on twenty goals for the 2007/08 season.

But then a call from Ajax changed everything.

CHAPTER 16

THE AJAX WAY

Luis had already been in Holland long enough to know Ajax's history. 'They've been European champions and they know how to help players improve,' he told Sofi one night as they waited for news on the ongoing talks between Groningen and Ajax. 'Who wouldn't want to go there?'

But his opinion didn't count and he felt helpless. Every few hours, his agent Daniel called with an update – sometimes good news, sometimes bad news. The move was on; then the move was off. By now, Luis was imagining life at Ajax and wanted the transfer to happen.

Finally, he got the official answer. 'Luis, you're going to be an Ajax player,' Daniel said, after a dramatic pause that made Luis's heart skip a beat. 'Don't expect any Christmas cards from Groningen after this whole mess, but they've accepted Ajax's offer.'

After the struggles when he started out in the Nacional first team, Luis knew there were no guarantees that he would be an instant hit at Ajax. 'There's a lot more pressure now,' he told Bruno once news of the transfer had spread. 'I'm going to miss you, but I just had to push for this opportunity. I hope you'll forgive me.'

Bruno understood. 'Luis, you're young and you've got the chance to be one of the best strikers in the world. How could I be angry with you?'

As soon as Luis walked into the Amsterdam Arena, Ajax's home stadium, he got goosebumps. Even with no fans there, it felt special. He looked down at the pitch and imagined himself scoring a winning goal with the crowd going crazy.

'I'm going to take this team to the next level,' he

told Ajax manager Henk ten Cate, as he received a
tour of the training ground.

Luis's confidence didn't please everyone, though.
Klaas-Jan Huntelaar wanted to be the team's star
striker too and he had dominated the previous
season. 'The Number 9 shirt is mine,' he told Luis,
with a smile. Luis couldn't tell if he meant the shirt
or the position as the lead striker, or both.

Luis was desperate to make a good first
impression. As he sat in the dressing room preparing
for his debut, he was happy to know that Sofi was
in the crowd. That would bring him luck. As kick-
off got nearer, Ten Cate walked over and shook
his hand. 'Don't try to do too much. Just show us
the same work rate and passion that you've always
played with. The goals will come.'

Luis made the perfect start. He set up the first
goal and scored the second himself. He ran over to
the Ajax fans and pointed to the name on the back of
his shirt – as if they needed reminding. The club had
spent a lot of money on Luis, and the fans wanted to
see if he was worth it. So far, they loved him.

But Luis's temper was always his worst enemy, both in the dressing room and on the pitch. Luis was always instantly sorry afterwards, but in the moment he would lose control.

One night, he called Sofi in tears. 'I've let everyone down again. Maybe I should just retire and forget about it all. I don't know what I was thinking. I guess I wasn't thinking. That's the problem.'

'Luis, you have to find a way to stay calm when you feel the anger coming,' she told him. 'But don't give up. Remember, you got to where you are because you have to win at all costs. You can't change who you are. If you didn't care as much, would you be playing for Ajax and chasing trophies, or would you be back in Montevideo working at a boring job and playing football in the street? It's easy to see all the negatives at the moment. But you'll find your way back. You always do.'

'I will. I'm one of the leaders at Ajax and the team needs me. But I just wish I was in the headlines for scoring goals instead of all these silly mistakes.'

As the months rolled on, Luis kept scoring but

his Ajax career was often shaky. When Marco van Basten, the legendary Dutch striker, was named as Ajax's new manager in 2008, Luis was delighted. 'Can you believe it?' he asked Paolo. 'I'm going to learn so much from him. If any manager is going to get the very best out of me, it's him.'

But that didn't go to plan either. On the pitch, he found the tactics confusing. Off the pitch, he hated all the team-building activities that were arranged. After a long afternoon of painting with his teammates, he vented his feelings to Gabri, a Spanish defender who had joined the club. 'We need to be working on things on the training ground, not sitting in a gallery with a paintbrush or doing treasure hunts. You can't force things – that's not how you create team spirit. Do you think PSV are doing this kind of nonsense?'

'I know,' Gabri admitted. 'It's not what I expected when I signed. It's supposed to bring us closer together as a team, but it's probably doing the opposite.'

'It's just as bad on the pitch. One week I'm

playing on the left, the next week I'm on the right. Then it's back to the left or in the centre. How am I supposed to play my best when I'm being moved around all the time? And why does he get so angry when I get yellow cards? It's part of the game,' Luis added.

When Van Basten left Ajax in 2009, Luis was disappointed not to have had more chances to learn from him, but was relieved to get a fresh start with a new manager, Martin Jol. In his heart, he still held that dream of playing for one of the top clubs in Europe. That meant moving to Spain, Italy or England. 'I think Jol is the man to get me there,' he told Daniel. 'Keep your phone with you at all times. I'm going to make sure people are asking about me.'

CHAPTER 17

CAPTAIN LUIS

'Luis, I want you to be our new captain,' Martin Jol explained as the two of them sat in his office after training. 'You make things happen for this team and the other players look up to you. I think you're ready for this.'

Luis said nothing at first. He was in shock.

'It's a great honour, thank you,' he managed finally. 'This is so exciting. I won't let you down.'

'I'll hold you to that,' Martin replied, with a big grin. 'We'll announce it to the rest of the players at the team meeting this afternoon. This is a new chapter for Ajax and we'll go as far as you can take us.'

Once the 2009/10 season started, Luis couldn't

stop scoring. 'I don't know if it's just the captain's armband, but I feel unstoppable,' he told Paolo one night. 'I can see the fear in defenders' eyes.' He began the season with a hat-trick in the second game and then scored four a few weeks later.

As Ajax captain, Luis had extra responsibilities and he was determined to get it right. He had made mistakes before, but this was his chance to show that he had learned from them.

'Since when did you get so grown up?' his teammates asked, noticing the change. 'What happened to the wild Luis?'

'I have to set an example now,' he would reply. 'The manager put his trust in me and I want to prove that he was right to give me the armband.'

He even had to give speeches in Dutch before the game. 'I'm going to keep it simple,' he told Martin. 'I'll just say we have to fight, work together and get the win.'

His teammates would laugh when Luis gave the same speech every week. 'Can't you think of anything else to say?' they joked.

'My speeches are working. That's what matters.'

They were working so well that Ajax reached the KNVB Cup Final in 2010. Luis even came up with a new speech to get the team fired up. 'This is our moment – just think about how it will feel to lift the trophy. Let's win the game and then we'll have a big party.'

Luis led the way to victory for Ajax with two goals in the second leg and then proudly walked up to collect the trophy. He kissed it, lifted it and then pumped his fist as the Ajax fans screamed even louder.

This was the happiest part of Luis's time at Ajax. He respected manager Martin, enjoyed the training sessions and loved the fans. Maybe he would stay in Amsterdam longer than he first thought.

But part of him still hoped that the big clubs were taking note.

'If you keep this up, this might be your last season in Holland,' Daniel told him at dinner one night during a visit to Amsterdam. 'I've even heard a few rumours about Barcelona tracking you, but I have no idea if they're true.'

Just hearing that there was a slight possibility of catching Barcelona's eye made Luis jump up from his chair. 'That's the dream,' he kept saying. Whenever he thought about playing in the Champions League Final, he imagined himself in either a Barcelona shirt or a Real Madrid shirt. There was just something so special about those teams.

He kept scoring but his goals weren't enough to clinch the Dutch title. Ajax finished second. 'Being runner-up hurts,' he told Sofi. 'I don't even want the medal. Put it in a box and leave it at the back of the wardrobe. I don't want to be reminded of this failure.'

'But this season was still your best ever,' Sofi reminded him. 'There wasn't a single defender in the league that could stop you. And you were a great captain. You should be proud of what you've achieved. Plus, you've got a big summer ahead.'

Luis smiled. Sofi was right. They had a baby girl on the way and Luis couldn't wait to become a father. But, before that, he was off to South Africa for the 2010 World Cup.

'The World Cup is the perfect distraction,' he told Sofi as he made his travel plans. 'Once I get there, I won't even think about missing out on the title. This could be a really great summer. How can I be miserable when I'm going to be playing in the greatest tournament in football? And then the baby will be here. That's going to be amazing. I can't wait to hold her in my arms.'

'I'll be cheering for Uruguay in every game ... but hurry back to us!' Sofi replied, with a wink.

As Luis waited for a taxi to the airport, his phone rang. It was Martin. 'Every kid dreams of playing in the World Cup, and you're about to do it,' he said, wishing Luis luck. 'The whole world is watching. Go and show people what a special player you are. Just don't expect me to cheer for you if you're playing against Holland!'

Luis laughed. He hadn't thought of that. 'If that happens, I'll just have to handle it.'

CHAPTER 18

THE HAND OF SUÁREZ

Luis missed many things about Uruguay – being with his family, eating his favourite food and watching Nacional every week, to name just three. But playing for the national team gave him the perfect chance to return home and show his love for his country. Now he had the 2010 World Cup to look forward to.

'Every prediction I've seen says Spain, Germany, Argentina or Brazil are going to be champions. No-one mentions Uruguay,' he moaned to teammates Diego Forlán and Edinson Cavani as they boarded the plane to South Africa.

'That's the way we like it,' Diego replied, rubbing

his hands together. 'We play our best when we're underdogs.'

Luis nodded. 'We can put all these predictions up in the dressing room, just for extra motivation. The media might not believe in us but we're going to surprise people.'

Uruguay had a strong team. They didn't have Lionel Messi or Xavi, but they had a solid game plan and the Suárez-Forlán-Cavani attacking trio was full of goals. When manager Óscar Tabárez, the man known as El Maestro, gathered his squad at the team hotel, he had a clear message: 'All of Uruguay is with us. We have to deliver for them. Play with passion, play with no fear and keep running until the final whistle. If we do all that, our talent will shine through.'

Luis didn't mind the hot weather, but he never enjoyed running laps of the pitch in training. He wanted the ball at his feet. 'Come on, let's get a game started,' he moaned during their first session in South Africa.

'Tough, Grumpy, you're all doing three laps first.'

'Whatever,' Luis muttered under his breath. Then

he started running. He loved to complain, but he always did what the coaches said.

Before long, everyone was calling him 'Grumpy'.

After a 0–0 draw against France in the first game, Luis couldn't sleep. He needed to play better or else Uruguay would be heading home and all the predictions would be proved right. 'That was our hardest game. We'll win our next two, you'll see,' he told Sofi on the phone that night, trying to sound more confident than he felt. On the pitch, he was giving it his all, but he called Sofi as often as he could, before and after training, for updates. 'Is the baby coming?' he asked each time.

'Not yet,' Sofi would reply. 'She's waiting for you to come home.'

Uruguay bounced back in the second game with a 3–0 win against South Africa. Luis charged into the box and was fouled for a penalty, and then he set up a goal for Álvaro Pereira. 'Nice cross,' Álvaro shouted, but Luis just looked confused and pointed to the crowd. It was impossible to hear anything with the sound of all the horns.

As Luis warmed up for the final group game against Mexico, he wanted a goal. Even when the team was winning, he hated not scoring. 'Stop hogging all the glory,' he told Diego, who had scored two in the last game. He was joking, but he wished he'd scored the goals instead.

When Edinson got the ball on the right wing, Luis sensed that this was his chance. Racing in from the left wing, he pointed to where he wanted the ball. 'Back post,' he screamed. The cross was perfect. Luis watched it arc over his marker and then timed his jump, heading the ball into the net. He ran to the Uruguay fans and let them join in the celebrations.

Uruguay had qualified for the next round. El Maestro hugged Luis at the final whistle, saying, 'El Salta! What a moment of magic!'

'I'm just getting started,' Luis replied, laughing. 'Wait till you see what I'm going to do next.'

South Korea looked like a tough opponent in the next round but Luis quickly saw weaknesses in its defence. He called to Diego: 'Just get the ball into the box – low and hard. I'll do the rest.'

Diego nodded back. Then he did as Luis
suggested. The goalkeeper couldn't reach the low
cross and Luis pounced to score from a tight angle.
'Wooooooooooooooooo,' he yelled, jumping on
Diego's back and pumping his fist.

When South Korea equalised, Luis was the first
one encouraging his teammates. 'There's still time.
We can do this,' he shouted.

Then a corner was cleared to Luis on the left
wing. Luis saw his defender hesitate. He darted
inside onto his right foot but saw other defenders
closing in. He didn't have time for more touches. He
had to shoot. He took a second to look at the goal,
and then curled a shot off the inside of the far post
and into the net.

As soon as he saw the net ripple, he sprinted
towards the Uruguay substitutes with his arms in the
air. His heart was racing and he just kept blowing
kisses to the Uruguay fans. With ten minutes to go,
that had to be the match-winning goal.

When the referee blew the final whistle, Luis fell
to the ground. He would never forget this night in

South Africa. Diego was the first to run over to him. 'You little genius,' he screamed, lifting Luis up.

Sofi and their baby – yet to be born – would have to wait a little longer for Luis's return. 'I wish I could be with you,' he told her that night. 'I really want to be there for our baby's birth.'

In the quarter-finals, it was Ghana standing between Uruguay and the semi-finals. 'This is the last African team left in the tournament – they have a whole continent cheering for them,' El Maestro explained. 'Most of the stadium will be cheering for them, so we're the underdogs. Give it everything you've got.'

At 1–1, with extra-time almost over, Ghana won a free-kick and Suárez ran back to help the defence. The commentators were already preparing everyone for a penalty shootout. The ball floated into the box and tired bodies jumped towards it. It all happened in an instant. Luis cleared the first header off the line, then the rebound bounced up and another header sent the ball zooming high towards the net. The goalkeeper was still on the ground after diving for the first header. Luis's instincts took over, and he made a great save, swatting the ball away with his hands. It was a clear penalty and a red card – but he had prevented a definite goal. Now Ghana had to score the penalty.

Luis couldn't watch. He stood on the touchline with the substitutes, covering his eyes with his shirt. Asamoah Gyan stepped up to take the penalty but his shot smacked against the top of the crossbar. Luis couldn't control himself. He was jumping up and down and running around like a madman.

'Luis, you saved our World Cup,' one of the substitutes said, putting an arm round him.

'I just did what I had to do,' Luis replied. When Uruguay won the penalty shootout to clinch a semi-final appearance against Holland, Luis sunk to his knees and kissed the pitch.

'I can't believe you did it, but what a save!' Diego said, giving Luis a soft punch on the shoulder. 'We owe you.'

'It was worth getting sent off to help us get through,' Luis agreed. But even as he joined in the celebrations, he could already feel the sadness building. He would be suspended for the semi-final, and he knew in his heart of hearts that – even though he had been acting on pure instincts – it had been unfair for Ghana to be knocked out this way, and he was sorry for that.

Edinson sensed it as they walked down the tunnel. 'Don't worry, Luis. We'll win the next one for you and you'll be back for the final.'

The next morning, Luis turned on the television in his room. The first thing he saw was a replay of his handball. People were calling him a cheat. They were calling his save 'the hand of the devil'. He saw posters where people had put a photo of his face with devil horns.

When he spoke to Sofi, he told her what he had just seen. She replied 'Well, in Uruguay there's a different reaction. I spoke to my friend and you are the King of Montevideo. You're a hero. There were parties everywhere. Even when you're not scoring goals, you still find a way to get the headlines!'

Luis felt more conflicted than ever. His country

had gone through, for which he was thankful, but he felt sorry for how it had come about.

Luis had to sit in his tracksuit for the semi-final, unable to help his teammates. It was agony. Holland were just too strong and he kept wondering if he would have made the difference. Luis jumped up every few minutes to shout encouragement, but it didn't help. Uruguay lost 3–2 and Luis had to accept that the dream was over. It had been a roller-coaster ride over the past few weeks. Uruguay had stunned the football world with their winning run and Luis had managed to be the hero and the villain at the same time.

Overall, he felt proud as he packed his bags. The World Cup journey had come to an end, and now all he could think about was rushing home to be with Sofi. 'I can't miss the birth,' he told Diego. 'I have to make it back in time.'

And he did. When Luis arrived home, he left his suitcase in the hallway and sat down on the sofa next to Sofi. He was so tired. 'I'm going to sleep well tonight,' he said, yawning.

A few weeks later, in the middle of the night, Luis woke suddenly as Sofi tapped his shoulder. 'Wake up!' she shouted. 'It's starting. The baby's coming!'

They rushed to the hospital. Later that day, little Delfina was born and Luis held her in his arms. He couldn't stop looking at her. She was so tiny that he was worried he would drop her. His handball was still a hot topic of conversation, but Luis paid no attention to any of that as he enjoyed his first few days as a father. The future was looking bright.

CHAPTER 19

ANFIELD ARRIVAL

Luis could feel that his time in Holland was coming to an end, though he was very proud to score his hundredth goal for Ajax and earn a place in the club's record books. He just needed a change. He gave his all for the first half of the season, but in January 2011 his phone buzzed and the number for his new agent, Pere Guardiola, appeared. He felt a burst of excitement as he answered the call.

'Give me good news, Pere.'

'Okay, Luis. No more rumours, I promise. Ajax have accepted an offer from Liverpool. I know it's not Barcelona or Real Madrid, but this is a big club with lots of fans. You should think about it. They aren't in the Champions League at the moment but they're going to spend the money to qualify.'

'Sure,' Luis said. 'I love watching the Premier League and I think I could make a real difference for Liverpool. With Steven Gerrard setting me up, I'll break all kinds of records.'

He was back to the waiting game again. The clubs talked, the agents talked but Luis had to stay on the sofa, go to training and try to act like it was business as usual. Inside, he had so many emotions. His little daughter, Delfina, was just a few months old and he knew it could be a big change for her too.

Pere called with the latest update: 'Everything is looking good. But I want you to meet with Kenny Dalglish, the Liverpool manager. After that, you'll know whether this is the right move.'

Dalglish flew to Amsterdam and laid out the plan, with an interpreter passing on the message in Spanish. 'You're probably looking at the squad and wondering if we're good enough,' he told him. 'That's a fair question. This is a great club with a great history. We've been champions of Europe and we want to get back to those glory years. You're a big piece of the puzzle and we'll be adding more players this summer. Signing for Liverpool might feel like a gamble – and, in a way, it is. But I really believe that you can step into Fernando Torres' shoes and lead us back to the top.'

Pere started to explain that Luis would need some time to think about his decision, but Luis waved a hand. He didn't need more time. He knew what he wanted. He wanted to help Dalglish turn Liverpool into a feared club again. 'I want to be a Red,' he said, grinning. '2011 is going to be a great year.'

That night, Luis looked through newspaper cuttings of his best moments at Ajax. He felt terrible to be letting the fans down but it was the right time to move on. 'I'm really pleased for you,' Martin Jol said as Luis came in to empty his locker. 'But I'm sad for the club. You'll always be part of the history here and I've enjoyed working with you as much as any player I've ever coached.' Before Luis could say anything, he was wrapped up in a big bear hug.

Luis and Sofi talked for hours as they prepared to

move to England. Sofi had researched all the local restaurants and supermarkets. They would stay at a hotel for the first few weeks, and then find a house to move into. 'We're leaving just as our Dutch was getting good,' Sofi said, laughing. 'I hope you're ready to go back to the classroom to learn English.'

Luis rolled his eyes. 'As long as I'm scoring goals, I'm sure the Liverpool fans won't care what language I'm speaking.'

When the plane landed in Liverpool, Luis opened his eyes, packed up his bag and took a deep breath. This was really happening. The boy who had learned the game on the streets of Montevideo was signing for another of Europe's most famous clubs.

Bruno had been there to help Luis and Sofi settle in Holland. Now, they were on their own in a new city – and that brought lots of challenges.

'Fella, yer can go in front of us in the queue, like,' an old man said as they waited to show their passports.

Luis felt the panic build inside him. He looked at Sofi for help. But for once she too was confused.

'Can you repeat that?' she asked the man.

'Yer can go in front,' he repeated, pointing.

Luis watched Sofi concentrating hard on the man's words. Suddenly, her eyes flickered. 'Oh, in front. Thanks.'

It would take many months before Luis learned enough English words to feel confident speaking to reporters, and even longer before he could understand the local accent. In the meantime, he relied on his Liverpool representative, Rod, and his interpreter.

After a quick stop at their hotel, there was only one place Luis wanted to go. 'Anfield,' he said with a huge smile.

His interpreter explained that was exactly where they were going.

As the car got closer to the stadium, Luis felt the butterflies in his stomach. Then he started seeing red everywhere. There were crowds of Liverpool fans outside the stadium, all there for a glimpse of the new signing. Him. Luis couldn't believe it. What would it be like for an actual Premier League match? He got out of the car slowly – half in shock, half taking his time to soak up the scene. He waved to the fans, then stopped to sign autographs and pose for photos.

It was only his first day in England, but the warm welcome had left him shaking. Then Kenny Dalglish appeared. The Liverpool manager had an even bigger grin than Luis had. 'Here's the goal machine!' he said. 'Welcome to Liverpool Football Club. We're thrilled to have you here.'

Luis shook his hand and tried out the few English words he knew. 'Thank you. Very happy for this moment.'

Then it was time to meet his new teammates. Again, Luis worried about the language barrier. Would he be able to explain how excited he was and how much he wanted to win a trophy with them?

Kenny kept everything simple for him. 'I'll introduce you to Stevie first. Then he can handle the rest of the introductions.'

Luis knew all about Steven Gerrard. That was a big part of the reason he was there.

'We're going to win a lot of games together,'

Stevie said, shaking Luis's hand. 'We've had some tough years but new signings like you will give us a chance to get back into the top four.'

Then Kenny was back, waving for Luis to join him. 'It's time for the photos with the Liverpool shirt. We know you want the Number 7 shirt – and that was our plan too. There's a great history of players wearing that shirt here. I wore it myself.'

'A long, long time ago,' Stevie added, teasing Kenny.

As Luis stood on the famous Anfield pitch, holding the Liverpool shirt for the cameras, he didn't need to be told to smile. He had a huge grin plastered all over his face. Now he just had to prove to everyone that he was worth the big price tag.

Luis was named in the squad to play Stoke that weekend, but he would be on the bench. When he heard the news, he was angry. 'They bought me to score goals. How can I do that if I'm a sub?' he moaned to Pere.

'Luis, you've just arrived and you're still learning about English football. This takes some of the pressure off.'

He was calmer by the time the game started. He jogged up and down the touchline and the Liverpool fans cheered him non-stop. The atmosphere was incredible, and lots of fans had already bought the 'Suárez 7' shirt. With about thirty minutes left, Kenny pointed to Luis. He was coming on. He threw off his tracksuit. The stadium announcer confirmed the substitution and the crowd roared. Luis had played in front of some loud crowds, but this was the loudest of all.

Stevie and Dirk Kuyt gave him high fives as he joined the action, saying, 'We'll get the ball up to you. Just be ready.'

The fans cheered every touch and every tackle. Even when he tried a backheel which didn't work, they clapped the idea. Then Dirk got the ball in space. He looked for Luis straight away, with a ball over the defence. Luis sprinted ahead of the defenders and knocked the ball to the left of the Stoke goalkeeper. The crowd was screaming, then suddenly they went quiet as they waited for Luis to shoot. The net was empty but the angle was tight. He took his time and fired in a shot. A Stoke defender tried to clear it off the line but the ball trickled into the net. Luis had done it.

He raced over to the fans, sliding on his knees and pumping his fist. 'Yeahhhh!' he screamed. Stevie hugged him. 'It took you fifteen minutes and the fans already love you.'

Joining mid-season didn't give Luis enough time to chase the Premier League title, but he helped them climb the table and finish sixth. 'We played well at the end of the season,' he told Maximiliano when he visited Luis in England. 'But it really hurts that we won't be in the Champions League next year.'

'You must be losing your touch,' Maximiliano teased. 'I thought you'd only need a few months to get Liverpool to the top of the table.'

Luis smiled and shrugged. 'Well, it's a tough league – tougher than I thought. There are no easy games, and Manchester United, Manchester City and Chelsea have such strong squads. But we can do much better. If we can get a few more new players, I think next season can be our year.'

CHAPTER 20

COPA AMÉRICA CHAMPION

'Why do they even call it a summer break?' Sofi asked, with a smile. 'There are still just as many games!'

Luis gave her a hug as he packed his bag ready for the 2011 Copa América in Argentina. 'I know it's not easy, but it's just three weeks. Then I'll be back.'

He felt bad to leave Sofi alone to look after Delfina, but his country needed him. 'We shocked the world last summer,' he told Edinson Cavani. 'Now we have to shock South America. People still think Argentina and Brazil are the favourites.'

From the very first training session with his teammates, Luis felt good. In training, every shot from every angle found the net. 'Luis, give the goalkeepers a chance,' El Maestro, the manager, shouted, with a big smile on his face. 'Save some for the tournament.'

Cheered on by thousands of Uruguay fans who had travelled to Argentina, Luis and his teammates earned a place in the quarter-finals – against Argentina. 'Now we have to beat Messi in front of his own fans,' El Maestro said calmly. 'If anyone can do it, we can.'

After 120 minutes, the game was locked at 1–1. A penalty shootout would decide it. El Maestro gathered the players on the pitch to confirm who would take the penalties. Luis's hand shot up straightaway. 'I want one,' he said confidently. Now he had to score it.

Messi scored. Diego scored. Luis was taking Uruguay's second penalty. He walked slowly towards the empty penalty area and placed the ball carefully on the spot. He took five steps back for a run-up and then took a deep breath. I know where I'm hitting this and the goalkeeper won't stop it, he told himself.

He hit his shot firmly. The Argentina goalkeeper guessed the right way but Luis had lifted the ball just enough. It fizzed into the net. He felt a mix of relief and joy as he raised his arm to celebrate. He rejoined his teammates on the halfway line. 'Great penalty,' Diego said, slapping him on the back.

When Uruguay keeper Fernando Muslera saved Carlos Tevez's penalty, Luis wanted to run over to hug him. But the game wasn't finished. Finally, it came down to Martín Cáceres. If he scored, Uruguay were into the semi-finals. Luis could hardly watch. When the ball hit the back of the net, the celebrations began. Luis took off his shirt as he sprinted across to Martín and Fernando.

El Maestro walked into the dressing room with his arms up. 'Wow! Just wow! Let's enjoy this moment, but we've got unfinished business. We're into the semi-finals. Argentina are out, Brazil are out. This is our tournament now. Let's finish the job.'

Everyone cheered. Luis got changed slowly. He wanted to enjoy this moment for as long as possible. As the players headed for the team bus, he saw hundreds of Uruguay fans singing and dancing. This win was for them.

'It was incredible – one of my best moments in football,' he told Sofi when she called later that night. 'But now I need to do even more. The team is counting on me to score the goals.'

'And you will. I can feel it. I have some extra incentive for you too. If you get to the final, Delfina and I will be there to cheer you on. We've already found plane tickets.'

Luis's heart jumped. He missed them so much and he always played well when Sofi was watching. 'That would be amazing. You have to see all the Uruguay fans here. It's crazy.'

At kick-off in the semi-final, Luis could think of nothing except reaching the final. His motto was always 'It's not that I want to win; it's that I *have* to win' – and it was especially true against Peru. 'Work your magic and make me a chance – I'll score it,' he had told the midfielders as they left the dressing room. And they delivered.

First, a low shot from outside the box created the

chance. Luis's eyes lit up as Peru's goalkeeper dived but could only push the ball out. In an instant, Luis pounced on it and poked a quick shot under the keeper and into the net.

Luis wasn't done. Moments later, a lobbed pass went over the heads of the Peru defenders, putting Luis one-on-one against the goalkeeper. He knew what he wanted to do. As the goalkeeper raced out, Luis knocked the ball to the side and then, even with his heart racing, calmly rolled the ball into the net.

'You beauty!' Diego screamed in his ear as they ran towards the Uruguay fans. 'We're going to be in the final.'

At the final whistle, the Uruguay players huddled in the centre circle, with lots of hugs and smiles. 'We've come this far, now we've got to lift the trophy,' Luis said. 'Let's do it for these fans!'

The next day, two more fans arrived. There was a knock on Luis's hotel room door and, when he opened it, Sofi was standing there smiling, holding little Delfina. 'You're here! This is turning into the best week ever,' he told her.

'And it'll be even better when you beat Paraguay in the final!' Sofi replied, as Delfina explored the hotel room.

As the Uruguay players jogged between cones on the pitch as part of the warm-up, El Maestro pulled Luis aside, saying, 'This is your moment. You've been the star of the tournament but now you've got to deliver in the final. Paraguay have played extra-time in the last two rounds. Their defenders will be tired so keep chasing them.'

Luis nodded and winked. He was ready. As soon as the game started, he knew El Maestro was right. The Paraguay defenders looked really tired. Luis felt stronger and quicker as he brushed them aside. Every time he got the ball, he thought he would score.

His big moment came in the first half. He controlled the ball on the right side of the penalty area, cut back onto his left foot and drilled a low shot into the far corner. It clipped the inside of the post and rolled over the line. Uruguay were ahead. Luis sprinted off to the corner flag, kissing his wrist and waving his fingers like pistols. He suddenly remembered that Sofi and Delfina were there. It felt even better to know that they had seen him score such an important goal.

Luis was a blur throughout the game. One minute he was chasing a defender on the right wing, then he was back on the left wing winning a corner. Diego made it 2–0 and Luis began thinking about lifting the Copa América trophy. He had one more trick up his sleeve. Uruguay won the ball and suddenly it was Luis and Diego against one Paraguay defender. The pass to Luis was perfect. He cushioned a clever header for Diego and then watched as his good friend fired in the third goal. Game over.

'You did it! Champions of South America!' Sofi yelled, hugging Luis. Luis picked up Delfina and carried her around the pitch. Finally, it was time to receive the trophy. Luis patiently waited his turn, then picked it up, kissed it and raised it high above his head. 'Yeahhhhh!' he screamed. He got his hands on another trophy five minutes later when he was announced as Player of the Tournament. 'This is for you!' Luis told Sofi afterwards. 'I couldn't do any of this without you.'

The party went on late into the night as the players celebrated with their families. Luis had always believed that he belonged on the biggest stages playing against the best players. Now he had the trophies to prove it.

CHAPTER 21

MAKING A MARK

Luis's second season in England was solid, but he knew he could do better. He helped Liverpool win the Carling Cup but the team finished eighth in the Premier League and his temper continued to land him in trouble. Most of all, he was desperate to play on the biggest European stage of all. 'I wish we were in the Champions League,' he told Paolo that summer. 'I'll just have to be patient, but I really want to test myself against the best.'

It was in his third season at Anfield, under new manager Brendan Rodgers, that Luis really took off. He had an instant connection with Brendan and his quick, attacking style of football.

'Get Luis the ball and he'll do the rest,' Brendan told the squad before the first game of the season. It became the motto for the year, and even Luis liked to repeat it.

With better crosses and more accurate passes, Luis couldn't stop scoring. He scored three against Norwich and three against Wigan. Maybe it wasn't such a hard league after all. The fans were loving it and every home game was extra noisy. By February, he had fifteen league goals to his credit.

One morning at training, Luis was firing shots from the edge of the penalty area when Liverpool goalkeeper Pepe Reina wandered over. Pepe stood next to the goal while he put on his gloves and said, 'On TV this morning, they were saying you could win the Golden Boot this season, Luis. You're right up there with Van Persie.'

Luis grinned. He had already thought about that and was keeping an eye on the rankings. 'That's why I've got to keep scoring. I want thirty or thirty-five.'

But just when it seemed as though Luis had settled in England and had put the bad days behind him, his temper got him in trouble again – this time when playing against Chelsea.

'Play it through!' he screamed, sprinting ahead of Chelsea defender Branislav Ivanović and pointing to where he wanted the pass. The ball was played through and the two players battled for it, pulling shirts and grabbing arms. Ivanović won the battle but as Luis saw the ball trickling away, he was bursting with anger. Before he could stop himself, he rushed in and committed a bad foul on Ivanović, who yelled to the referee.

It was Luis's lucky day. No-one had noticed and the game carried on. He even managed to score a late goal to get Liverpool a 2–2 draw. But in the dressing room afterwards, there were no celebrations. He knew a punishment was coming.

'Cheer up, Luis!' Stevie called from across the room. 'Your goal just got us a point.'

'Thanks! But we didn't win.' Luis couldn't face talking about the incident yet and most of his teammates hadn't seen it.

'We can't win them all,' Stevie replied.

Well, *I* have to, Luis thought. Winning was the whole point of playing.

'Seriously, Luis,' Stevie said, walking over and putting an arm round his teammate. 'What's wrong? You've barely smiled since we got back in here.'

Luis looked at the floor and shook his head. 'I've let everyone down.'

'What do you mean?'

'You'll see tonight,' he said, picking up his bag and walking to his car.

Sure enough, Luis was all anyone wanted to talk about. Some people were saying that Liverpool should just let Luis leave. Reporters found all the old stories from Holland about his temper, and Luis didn't leave the house for three days.

When a ten-match suspension was announced, Luis put his hands over his face. 'I can't believe this is happening again,' he told Sofi as she tried to comfort him. 'Everyone has been so good to me – the other players, the fans, the coaches – and this is how I repay them. I was having a great season and now this is all anyone will remember. I just wish everyone knew how sorry I am.'

There was nothing he could do about the suspension, but he wanted to do the right thing. Pere managed to get Ivanović's phone number. Luis sat down on the sofa, took a deep breath and began dialling.

'Hello?' said the voice on the line.

'Hi Branislav, it's Luis Suárez,' he explained. 'Look, I know I'm the last person you want to speak to, but I had to call. I had a moment of madness and I'm very sorry.'

'It was such a weird game. Why did you do it?'

'I lost control. It's stupid but that's the truth. I was angry that we weren't winning.'

'Look, I accept your apology. Let's just forget it and move on.'

It felt good to hear Branislav say that, but this wasn't how it was meant to be. Luis had thought moving to England would give him a chance to be a champion, but that plan was backfiring badly. As he sat in the crowd and faced his suspension, he had so many doubts. The biggest one was whether he even had a future at Liverpool.

CHAPTER 22

CHASING THE TITLE

With the 2013/14 season just weeks away, Luis's future at Liverpool was still in doubt. Arsenal had made a bid to sign him and he loved the idea of playing Champions League football, but Liverpool rejected it. Other teams were also rumoured to be interested. It was like the Ajax transfer all over again – days of meetings, lots of newspaper stories and he was just sitting at home helplessly.

'Another photographer followed us to the park,' Luis told Sofi angrily. 'I can't go anywhere without someone putting a camera in my face.' He slumped down on the sofa and questioned his future in England for the hundredth time that week.

Reading his mind, Sofi asked: 'Can you face a full season of this? I've seen what it's done to you. If you decide you need a fresh start, I will support you one hundred per cent.'

Luis smiled. He hadn't done a lot of that lately. 'My angel, what did I do to deserve you?' he said, stroking her hair. 'Let's see how the next few weeks go. Moving to Italy or Spain sounds like a tempting idea at the moment, but I don't want to be known as a player who runs away as soon as things get difficult.'

Things quickly got worse. Brendan stopped Luis from training with the first team. When he heard his manager's decision, Luis just took a ball to the far side of the training ground. He had nothing left to say.

Stevie found Luis practicing free-kicks on his own one afternoon. He walked over and the two players sat together on the grass. Stevie wanted to get his points across before it was too late. 'I understand why other top clubs are interested and I see why you would want to play there. I've been through all that myself. But these fans deserve to be back in the Champions League and winning titles again. Together, we can make it happen. I know you and your family have been through a lot. Just promise me that you'll think about it.'

Luis nodded. Stevie was the most talented teammate he had ever had, and one of the nicest too. It was another reminder that he could become a Liverpool legend if he stayed and helped the team beat the likes of Manchester United and Chelsea. As the season began, he was out of the team and had to watch from the crowd. The Anfield crowd sang 'You'll Never Walk Alone' and Luis felt even sadder that he wasn't on the pitch.

Sitting next to her husband, Sofi turned to Luis and looked him in the eye. 'It's time.'

He nodded. He was a footballer. That's all he knew. It didn't matter if he would be at Liverpool next year, or the year after. He had a contract for this season and he owed it to the fans and his teammates to do his best for the club. After the game, he went down to Brendan's office. 'Can we talk?' he asked.

Brendon waved him in. 'We missed you out there

today. We scored one, but you'd have scored four.'

Luis grinned. He knew it was true. Liverpool had missed some easy chances. 'Let's work through this. I want to be back out there. What do you need from me?'

'First, I want you to understand that all of this has been about what's best for Liverpool. I like you, Luis. I always have. You're a fantastic player. But I wouldn't be doing my job if I'd let you walk away.'

'I know. This summer has been a nightmare and I could have done things differently. All I care about is getting back on the pitch and helping the team.'

'Great. This could be an amazing year. We've started well and we're going to be even better once you're back.'

Luis stood up and shook Brendan's hand. 'Let's go and win a title,' he said, smiling all the way to the door.

With Luis back in the team, Liverpool transformed from defensive and scrappy to attacking and explosive. He was determined to make everyone forget about the past six months. 'Scoring goals is the best way,' Stevie told him. 'Just go out and tear defences apart.'

Week after week, that's what Luis did. He scored two against Sunderland then a hat-trick against West Brom. He saved something even more special for Norwich – he got four, each one more spectacular than the last. Even in the warm-up, he felt the ball flying off his foot. 'Save some for the game,' Stevie joked. Luis winked. He had plenty up his sleeve.

Early in the first half, he picked up a loose ball thirty yards out, saw the Norwich keeper off his line and looped a perfect lob into the net. Before he was done, he added an unstoppable volley and a beautiful free-kick. Even he couldn't believe it as he ran off to celebrate each time.

By Christmas, the Suárez story had taken a surprising twist. 'They're predicting that I'll win Footballer of the Year,' he told Sofi. He was proud of that – and equally proud that his English was now good enough that he could read the newspapers.

'I should have bet on you in August,' Sofi said.

'No-one would have believed it back then. Maybe little Benjamin is your lucky charm.'

Luis grinned. His second child, Benjamin, was only a few months old but he already had a special place in Luis's heart.

Suddenly, Liverpool were title contenders, and Luis was dragging his teammates along. Every time they needed something special, he was there to provide it. 'The fans can taste it,' Luis told Lucas as they warmed up for a huge game against Chelsea. 'If we win today, we are one step closer. It's the last big test.'

But the pressure got to all the Liverpool players. Luis struggled to produce his usual magic, and then Stevie slipped at the worst possible moment. 'Oh no,' Luis said under his breath as Chelsea took the lead. He could feel the panic in the crowd. For once, he couldn't rescue the team.

'It's not over,' he said loudly in the dressing room after the game, as the players sat quietly, heads in their hands. 'Until the league table says that Manchester City are champions, we have a chance.'

Three days later, Luis had to accept that the

dream had slipped through his fingers. Liverpool took a 3–0 lead against Crystal Palace, but threw it away to draw 3–3. Every Palace goal was like a dagger in his chest. As the reality started to sink in, Luis felt numb. Then, even before he reached the dressing room, he burst into tears. Brendan tried to console him, but all Luis could say was: 'After all the hard work, we blew it.'

It took Luis a long time to recover from this disappointment, but one happy moment came in London at the end of season awards night. His spectacular season had not gone unnoticed. After all the negative headlines, he was being recognised for the right reasons again. When his name was called out for the Player of the Year award, he was shaking. It meant so much after some difficult months in England.

'I always try my best for the team and it is nice to get awards,' he explained on accepting the trophy, 'but really this is for my teammates and the staff at Liverpool because without their help I wouldn't have this prize.'

Later that evening, Chelsea manager José Mourinho walked over to Luis, shook his hand and congratulated him on the award. 'You really deserve that. Very few players could have bounced back like you did. You're a fighter.'

Now, after a season of highs and lows, Luis just wanted to get back on the pitch and score more goals. As he joined his Uruguay teammates in Brazil for the 2014 World Cup, he was counting the days until the first match.

CHAPTER 23

WORLD CUP HIGHS AND LOWS

The room was silent. Players threw their boots in the middle and headed for the showers. The World Cup had only just begun but Uruguay had lost to Costa Rica, the weakest team in their group. Luis had tried everything to shake off a knee injury, working day and night with the physio, Walter Ferreira. But it was no good. He couldn't run and he had to watch the game from the dugout.

Edinson tapped Luis on the shoulder as they headed to the bus for a miserable journey back to the hotel. He looked pale. 'Grumpy, we need you. Is there any chance you'll be back for the England game?'

Luis wasn't sure. He had more tests planned for the next morning and the physio had told him it was a 50–50 chance. 'I don't care what anyone says, I'm playing,' he replied quietly. 'More than that, I'm going to give the English reporters another Suárez story to write about.'

Edinson smiled. 'Good. I can sleep tonight now.'

Three days later, Luis kept his word. He didn't know how his knee would react, but he was back. He could hear the Uruguay fans screaming. His chest was thumping. Playing in a World Cup in South America was a dream come true, and it was all the sweeter that the game was against England.

As he shook hands with Stevie, they exchanged a wink. 'Good luck,' Luis said. Stevie was his friend but for the next ninety minutes he was the enemy. Luis jogged to the centre circle and his mind was completely focused on winning the game for Uruguay.

Just before half-time, he saw his first chance. Luis saw Edinson make a clever run on the left and instinctively knew that the ball would go to the back post. He peeled away from his marker and Edinson's cross was perfect. It sailed straight to Luis and he angled a header down into the far corner. 1–0. After the pain of missing the first game, he let all his emotion show.

When England equalised, it seemed that Uruguay were sliding to another defeat. But Luis refused to let that happen. He was feeling pain in his knee with every step, but his brain was working just fine. He saw a long pass and gambled that the ball would be flicked on. While the England defenders waited, Luis had already made his move. It was actually Stevie who accidentally headed the ball backwards. Luis was through on goal but he felt his legs getting weaker. He had to get a shot in quickly before the defenders could recover. 'Shoot!' the Uruguay fans screamed. Luis wound back his right foot and thumped the ball as hard as he could. It flew like a rocket past the goalkeeper and into the top corner.

He saw the ball hit the back of the net, but he just kept running, arms in the air. He raced over to Walter who had given up so much time to help

Luis get back on the pitch. It had all been worth it. Uruguay hung on for the win, and Luis grabbed the match ball. 'I want this for my collection,' he told the referee, grinning.

Back in the dressing room, Luis turned the music up loud and the celebrations continued. The loss to Costa Rica was forgotten. 'We're back on track,' El Maestro told his players. 'But we still need to win the next game. It's knockout football all the way now.'

The final game against Italy would decide who reached the second round. 'It doesn't get much bigger than this,' one of the coaches said. 'If we keep our heads and play our best, we can do it. Luis, I hope you saved something special for this game.'

Luis smiled. He liked that everyone looked to him for a bit of magic. He saw the passion of the Uruguay fans at training, around the cities, back home and at the games. He was determined to win for them.

But Italy needed to win too. Their defenders bumped and grabbed Luis from the very first whistle, doing their best to throw him off his game. His

teammates couldn't get the ball to him and he felt
the frustration growing.

Then he snapped. Italy defender Giorgio Chiellini
was battling Luis for position in the box, with all
the usual pushing and shirt pulling. But when he
couldn't win the ball, the anger took over. Before he
could calm himself down, he took out his frustration
on Chiellini with another foul. Instantly, he knew he
was in trouble.

He fell to the ground and prayed that the referee
hadn't seen it. But he was out of luck. He sat up to
see the red card pointed in his direction. His World
Cup had ended in controversy again.

Luis sat in the dressing room crying. This was
his worst nightmare. At least the handball in 2010
had been for the good of the team. This was just a
selfish moment of madness. He could barely watch
the second half as Uruguay scrapped their way to a
1–0 win. They were through to the second round,
but Luis's tournament was over. In the space of a
few days, he had gone from national hero to global
villain. Everyone suddenly had an opinion about him.

That night, after thirty minutes of trying to sleep, he gave up. His mind was racing and he couldn't get comfortable. He wanted to turn on the television but he knew they would just be showing replays of the incident. Instead, he paced around the room. It was a familiar feeling for Luis – the embarrassment and the sadness, plus he was worried about how serious his punishment might be. He just kept asking himself: 'Why? Why? Why?'

It was going to be a long summer.

CHAPTER 24

BOUNCING BACK IN BARCELONA

When he got the call, he was sitting on the bed getting ready to go for a run. He would always remember everything about that moment. It was a good thing that he was sitting down because the news would have knocked him over. A decision had been made on his suspension – he would be banned from football for four months, and it even included training.

'Four months?' he yelled. 'This time away from football is going to be so hard,' he told Sofia with regret in his voice. 'But I know I made a mistake. The best way for me to show everyone that I've learned my lesson is to accept the punishment and make sure it never happens again.'

Football and his family were his life. Now one of them had been taken away. What was he supposed to do every day? He had heard about the suspension five minutes ago and he already felt the panic. How was he going to manage four months?

'Just take it one day at a time,' he told himself.

Most of all, he wanted everyone to know how sorry he was. He knew Liverpool would be furious. They were losing their best player for months for something that happened while Luis was playing for Uruguay.

At Anfield, Brendan Rodgers saw the announcement and shook his head. The team had come so close to winning the title but it was all in danger of falling apart. His phone rang and he knew it would be his bosses.

'Enough is enough. Suárez has dragged this club through nightmare after nightmare. He's let us down and he's let the fans down. He's a brilliant player, no question, but it's time for him to go. We'll listen to offers.'

Rodgers knew that was coming. 'Understood.'

The next day in Spain, Luis's ban was again the

topic of conversation. But Barcelona saw things differently. Various opinions were voiced by the team's management:

'He's a handful and he loses control sometimes, but the fact is he's the best goalscorer in the world. Even though he is clearly sorry for his actions, everyone is turning their back on him. That feels like an opportunity to me.'

'But can he really be a Barcelona player after all the incidents? We talk about being 'més que un club' [more than a club] and we're sponsored by UNICEF. It would be a nightmare for our image. We'll get a lot of criticism.'

'That's all true. But we have to consider making an offer. Put him alongside Messi and Neymar and we'll score five a game. You know Real Madrid will be having this same conversation right now. Do we want to see Suárez and Cristiano Ronaldo team up? We want to win back the Champions League and he could be the difference. We love to pass, pass, pass but sometimes you need a poacher too. With Suárez, it's shoot, shoot, shoot.'

'Let me just say this,' a third voice added. 'He has apologised. He knows he made a mistake and he has been punished for it. But doesn't everyone deserve a second chance? Put him on a team that already has Messi, Iniesta and Xavi, and he'll be incredible. He's surrounded by the best players in the world.'

A conversation that was supposed to last fifteen minutes went on and on. By midnight, they had reached a decision. They would take a chance and make an offer for Luis.

The next day, Rodgers raised his eyebrows as he looked over all the paperwork. 'I didn't expect Barcelona to be the team that wanted him,' he said. They had gathered to discuss a big money offer that would allow Liverpool to move on and rebuild. There were nods all around the table. It was going to be a short meeting.

Luis danced around the room when Pere told him that Liverpool had accepted Barcelona's offer. He couldn't even join them for training yet, but it would be worth the wait. He was going to the Nou Camp to play with Messi.

While their children, Delfina and Benjamin, played on the sofa, Sofi raised a glass of champagne and smiled at Luis. 'Congratulations, darling. It's your dream move. And we'll be close to my parents so they'll be able to help with the kids.'

'I couldn't have done any of it without you,' he replied. 'Thank you for always standing by me.'

As Luis packed up the last box, he looked around their empty house. His time at Liverpool had been a roller-coaster ride, with some very good moments and some very bad ones. It was still sad to leave.

Just then, his phone rang. It was a number he didn't recognise.

'Hello?' he answered.

'Hey Luis, it's Leo Messi,' was the reply. Luis was stunned. Messi had his phone number? 'We're all looking forward to having you at Barcelona. You're going to score a lot of goals and we're going to be unstoppable.'

'It's going to be an honour,' Luis replied. 'I can't wait.'

He was already picturing it all – Messi darting past

three defenders, then playing the perfect pass for Luis to score. Messi liked to create goals; Luis loved to score them.

Luis wasn't sure how the Barcelona fans would react. They would know all of his history and he wouldn't even be able to play until October. But all he saw was overwhelming support. They cheered him, wanted to take photos with him and wished him luck for the season. He just wanted to repay them by scoring goals straight away. Instead, all he could do was watch tapes of training and do his own workouts.

'They're all so good,' he told Paolo as they ate tapas at a restaurant by the beach. 'Even the defenders are really skilful.'

'Luis, as soon as you're back they'll see that you're the best striker in the world. Only you could go through all of that drama and still end up as Barcelona's new striker.'

Finally, the suspension came to an end and Luis could think about helping the team win trophies. 'I've got a real advantage,' he told Sofi that week.

'I might be a little rusty but I'm totally fresh. No

bumps, no bruises. I'm ready to make up for lost time.' After all the negative headlines, he was just happy that Barcelona had given him this chance.

As luck would have it, his Barcelona debut was an away game with rivals Real Madrid. All week, Luis trained hard and hoped to impress the coaches enough to earn a place in the squad. Even if he was only ninety per cent fit, he felt he could be a dangerous weapon off the bench. Then Luis Enrique, the Barcelona boss, called Luis aside as they arrived at the stadium. 'You're in the starting line-up,' he said quietly. 'It's a bit of a gamble but we think you're ready. Just be honest with us when you start to feel tired.'

Luis was speechless. He would be making his debut as the central striker alongside Leo and Neymar.

It was one of the biggest games of the season and he couldn't wait. As he stood in the tunnel, he thought about all the times that he had dreamed of playing for Barcelona, even long before the transfer actually happened. Now he was wearing the number 9 shirt and hoping to score his first goal for the club.

Luis only needed three minutes to make an

impact. His clever pass set up a goal for Neymar, and he instantly felt part of the team as they celebrated with the Barcelona fans. The night went downhill from there as Real Madrid fought back to win, but Luis's career in Spain was officially underway. 'This is going to be an incredible adventure,' he told Sofi when he called from his hotel room. 'Tonight wasn't the ideal result, but I think I'm going to win a lot of trophies with this team.'

He was right. Barcelona brushed aside the rest of Spain on their way to the La Liga title, and then lifted the Spanish Cup. Luis was in the thick of it all, scoring twenty-four goals despite missing the start of the season. 'Champions! Champions!' he sang, with one arm round Leo, the other round Neymar. They were an unstoppable trio. 'One more to go,' Leo said, reminding Luis that the Champions League final against Juventus was still to come.

'Bring it on!' Luis yelled. 'I love this winning feeling.'

'Winning the Champions League is the best feeling of all,' Leo said, grinning. 'So don't fluff it when I set you up.'

Luis couldn't stop thinking about the Treble. They had to beat Juventus – they just had to. The bus journey to the stadium was quieter than ever as the players took deep breaths before the battle ahead. Now, the waiting was finally over and he could feel the buzz around the stadium. He loved playing in big games. 'This is why I had to come to Barcelona,' he said quietly to himself.

The Champions League anthem played loudly as Luis walked out onto the pitch with his Barcelona teammates. He tried to savour every moment – the smells, the cheers, the feel of the pitch.

But he quickly saw that he was going to have a difficult evening, even after Barcelona took an early lead. The joyful celebrations faded as Luis struggled to make an impact on the game. The Juventus defenders marked him tightly and pulled his shirt again and again. Usually he could make clever runs behind the defence but today he was finding no space.

Suddenly, Juventus pulled level. With the score at 1–1, both teams were desperate to take control. 'This is my moment,' Luis muttered to himself. 'I can still be the hero and help us lift the trophy.' When Leo's shot was saved, Luis reacted quickest to put Barcelona ahead. He didn't even have time to think – it was pure instinct. He saw the ball bounce loose and he whipped a quick shot into the top corner past Juventus goalkeeper Gianluigi Buffon. When he saw the ball hit the back of the net, he raced off to celebrate, with all his teammates chasing him to join in the celebrations. Barcelona then added a third goal to seal the Treble – but it was Luis who had changed the game when it mattered most. 'We did it!' he screamed, jumping on Leo's back and waving a fist to the crowd.

Sofi clapped and clapped. What a year! Luis had said that Barcelona would be a fresh start. Now it was as if the World Cup heartbreak had never happened. She had never seen her husband smile so much.

'This is just the beginning,' Luis told her after the game as the players celebrated with their families. 'We're going to be even better next season. I still can't believe this journey – from Salto to Barcelona! And we've done it all together. It's a crazy dream, but I don't ever want to wake up from it!